T0248101

SLAVERY
AFTER
SLAVERY

SLAVERY
AFTER
SLAVERY

‑○‑○‑○‑○‑○‑○‑

REVEALING THE LEGACY OF
FORCED CHILD APPRENTICESHIPS
ON BLACK FAMILIES,
FROM EMANCIPATION TO
THE PRESENT

MARY FRANCES BERRY

BEACON PRESS, BOSTON

BEACON PRESS
Boston, Massachusetts
www.beacon.org

Beacon Press books
are published under the auspices of
the Unitarian Universalist Association of Congregations.

28 27 26 25   8 7 6 5 4 3 2 1

This book is printed on acid-free paper that meets the uncoated paper
ANSI/NISO specifications for permanence as revised in 1992.

Text design and composition by Kim Arney

Library of Congress Cataloging-in-Publication Data
Names: Berry, Mary Frances, author.
Title: Slavery after slavery : revealing the legacy of forced child apprenticeships
on Black families, from emancipation to the present / Mary Frances Berry.
Description: Boston : Beacon Press, [2024] | Includes bibliographical references. |
Summary: "An acclaimed historian narrates the stories of newly emancipated
children who were re-enslaved by white masters through apprenticeships
and their parents' fights to free them" —Provided by publisher.
Identifiers: LCCN 2024031817 (print) | LCCN 2024031818 (ebook) |
ISBN 9780807007839 (hardcover) | ISBN 9780807007846 (ebook)
Subjects: LCSH: Child labor—United States. | Apprenticeship programs—
Moral and ethical aspects—United States—History. | African American
children—Employment—Moral and ethical aspects—United States. | African
American apprentices—United States—Social conditions. |
Slavery—United States. | African Americans—History—19th century |
African Americans—History—1877-1964.
Classification: LCC HD6250.U3 B47 2025 (print) |
LCC HD6250.U3 (ebook) |
DDC 331.3/10973—dc23/eng/20240823
LC record available at https://lccn.loc.gov/2024031817
LC ebook record available at https://lccn.loc.gov/

To the memory of my slave ancestors
and all who were enslaved
on the Southall plantation in
Williamson County, Tennessee

CONTENTS

VIOLET MAPLE'S AMERICAN DREAM

iolet Maples's dream forever eluded her after emancipation from slavery. She could never gather her children, one of whom was biracial, and her brothers together when freedom came in 1865. They could not move from the Limestone County, Alabama, plantation on which they were born, and she could not afford to purchase some land where they might enjoy their freedom together. The law did not come to her aid. The son of Violet's slave owner's brother and a slave woman, George Bridgeforth, lived on his father's local plantation. George received consistent financial help from his father, and George's family and descendants prospered. They ended up living Violet's dream into the twenty-first century.

This book tells the story of Violet Maples and others after slavery. It describes the experiences and history of black families who tried to use the law to keep their children from being pulled back into slavery. Some succeeded and some failed.

Their stories are in many ways the story of my own family who had been slaves on a Southall plantation in Williamson County near Franklin, Tennessee, and one in Davidson County.

They, like many others of the formerly enslaved, took the slave owners' name—Southall—after Emancipation, and my mother's father, Charlie Southall, eventually became a tenant farmer. My grandmother Mattie died from giving birth to my mother, the youngest of twelve children. Then, when my grandfather Charlie died of uncontrolled diabetes, her siblings were left to support the family and raise my mother. They, like other families discussed in this book, survived by overcoming poverty, anti-black racism, and economic hard times. Through it all, these black families, like so many others, managed to maintain extended family ties and networks throughout the generations.

Today, Williamson County is one of the wealthiest areas in the United States. Franklin's attraction is not only its natural beauty but its proximity to Nashville. Country music stars, other stars, and those without stars pay no state income taxes; instead the sales tax burden, even for food and essentials, falls on consumers, especially harming the poor. The Southall label means a luxury resort and playground for wealthy tourists. The county's history, its economic reliance on slavery and the exploitation of black workers—even today—is largely unrecognized. No historical marker recalls the Southall African Americans slaves who lived, worked, and died there. Those who continue to be called Southall have been disconnected from this part of their past. These stories pay tribute to their resilience and struggles.

SLAVERY
AFTER
SLAVERY

PLUMB LINES

The stories in this book have all been drawn from decisions made by Southern courts in the years after the Civil War. All involve black children and youth entrapped by white adults. Most cases involve civil matters, primarily matters of habeas corpus, a legal term used to refer to illegal imprisonment but also to matters of child custody, apprenticeships, and indentures. Those were the terms used in the nineteenth century, but if these cases were tried today, prosecutors could draw on criminal law. We now might label these cases as trafficking at the most extreme: they involve minors who were made to labor for other adults against their will. They were moved across state lines and county lines, from one plantation to another, to do hard work, or even illegal work, which enriched the white people who controlled them.

The Thirteenth Amendment abolished slavery and what we now call human trafficking, and the federal Civil Rights Act of 1866 gave blacks the right to freely make contracts, including marriage. But the demands of agricultural production under capitalism required cheap labor, including that of children, and in a system where white supremacy was so ingrained that it was like the humidity of a Southern summer, white people believed that black people existed to do that work.

White planters refused to accept the meaning and spirit of abolition, and they strategized with their neighbors, their elected officials, and their lawyers over how to maintain control over black labor. The apprenticeship system, an ancient tradition that extended deep into English and European history, was commonplace in the American colonies and early United States as well. It was always exploitative, demanding years of unpaid "internships," but the idea was that after years of working for a master tradesman to learn a skilled craft, the apprentice could become a free individual and member of the guild. Famously, Benjamin Franklin was apprenticed as a printer in Philadelphia in the colonial era, though few remember that he ran away and escaped punishment for that crime. While white boys held most apprenticeships, local courts apprenticed poor or orphaned free Negro boys and girls in the antebellum era when they determined that the children might become a public charge. Slave emancipation in the Northern states occurred gradually, and slavery persisted for years in New York and New Jersey. New York ended slavery in 1827, but the last sixteen Northern enslaved African Americans were not freed until 1866 in New Jersey when the state ratified the Thirteenth Amendment. Until then they were called apprentices.[1]

White Southerners transformed apprenticeships after the war into a system that entrapped black children, youth, unmarried women, and their families into years of indentured servitude. Tenant farming, peonage, farm labor, and convict leasing ensured that black people remained bound to whites who controlled their labor and restricted their movements. In addition, Southern mills employed thousands of black women and children who labored for pittances in the dirtiest, roughest, and most dangerous jobs; the meagre legal protections granted to white female and child laborers did not extend to black women and children.[2]

Whites used the criminal justice system to punish black people and maintain white supremacy, as I have shown in earlier books (*Black Resistance/White Law* and *Pig Farmer's Daughter*). In contrast, the National Ex-Slave Mutual Relief, Bounty and Pension Association led by Callie House at the turn of the century, offered its three hundred thousand members the opportunity to envision recompense for slavery and a life free from debt bondage. A long line of scholars, including John Hope Franklin (whose family survived the 1921 Tulsa Race Massacre) and John Blassingame (a descendant of Georgia sharecroppers), as well as Pete Daniel and Edward E. Baptist, and journalists Douglas Blackmon and Isabel Wilkerson, among others, have documented whites' systemic deprivation of resources, wages, and pleasures to black people, while delighting us with tales of black resilience and those who managed to secure a bootstrap by which they pulled themselves up.

The reality of African American lives is too often an overabundance of everything that is harmful to the development of human capital: precarious work, environmental destruction, poor diet, negligent health care, under-resourced segregated schools, and prison systems. These are undeniable truths that even calls for the abolition of critical race theory in school curricula and the banning of books cannot erase. As the US Congress wavers on whether to move ahead with a national commission to study reparations, as H.R. 40, which would establish a commission to study and develop reparation proposals for African Americans, recommends, many remain uncertain about the need for such legislation. The court of public opinion is not convinced. Moreover, the US Supreme Court, though it has not ruled specifically on the issue, has raised the level of proof necessary to demonstrate illegal harm based on race. It seems that civil rights plaintiffs must prove a specific intent rather than a totality of circumstances that harm individuals before a judge may order any remediation at all. The court must also expect claims that reparations for descendants of African American slaves constitute preferential treatment and are therefore illegal.

Black farmers' long struggle for eventual recompense shows how well-crafted scholarly evidence can further policy change and persuade a court. It also shows how claims of racial preferences can impede seeming success. The 1982 report *The Decline of Black Farming in America*, by the US Commission on Civil Rights (USCCR), published while I was vice chair, documented the history of race discrimination against black farmers by the US Department of Agriculture. Department officials and their agents had systematically denied black farm owners crucial crop loans, delayed applications for relief, and purposely prevented access to educational resources that led to the rapid decline in the number of agricultural operations owned by African Americans. The report also documented the social and economic consequences of discrimination. A class action suit brought by black farmers against the USDA in 1999 drew on their experiences, as well as the USCCR report, securing a $1.25 billion judgment. Even then, it was not until 2013 that some plaintiffs in *Pigford v. Glickman* began receiving monetary awards. Further financial help for black farmers has been stalled.

It's possible to demonstrate that specific individuals and their descendants were systematically injured through white supremacist practices. This is why the stories I tell in this book are important. No discussion of reparative justice for the formerly enslaved should occur without including their experience. This harm is not timebound but has continuing effects. No statute of limitations applies, and Congress cannot claim sovereign immunity to deny the appropriation of funds.

I recognize that the narratives in this book are limited to specific families. Some researchers know of the cases discussed, but I have traced the black participants and their descendants into the late twentieth century to understand the impact of their experiences afterwards.[3] They illustrate the kind of lasting impact other black families have faced. Since marriages during slavery were not legally recognized, over two million of the about four million slaves in the 1860 population, between the ages of ten and nineteen, were likely subject to apprenticeships, easily labeled as without parental support. The Freedmen's Bureau (1865–1872) handled some claims and provided legal representation for a few families who lost their children. Financial barriers meant that very few objections ever reached the courts.[4]

Even when the small number of cases reached the appeals courts, justice depended upon timing. Judges who were ex-Confederates or sympathizers appointed during Andrew Johnson's Reconstruction usually decided against black plaintiffs, leaving children with their former slave master. Carpetbaggers, white Northern Republicans who came to the South after the American Civil War, and former Union officers appointed after Congress reconstructed the South starting in 1867 usually rendered decisions for the formerly enslaved parents. However, a Northerner judge could decide that children were better off economically with the planter than with a poor parent and deny parental custody. Inevitably, there are hundreds if not thousands of other stories of children thrown back into slavery that await future research. Meanwhile, these stories might provide additional understanding of the reparations question.

The institutionalization of racism enriched white plantation owners through the control of black people's labor. Yet the consequences of these decisions were more than economic: they reached far into the very bonds of family and personal relationships. The appropriation of black labor manifested in ways that have been largely overlooked as a source of inequality, reproducing dismal economic prospects and more far into the future. The results were emotional damage, loss of human potential, and intergenerational impoverishment. The legacy of racial prejudice that saw people of African descent as uncivilized, and therefore unfit for citizenship, continues to color American culture and social policies; the black youth pipelined into prison systems ensure white control is maintained. Mere actuarial science cannot calculate these losses.

This work examines the history of families, focused on those who challenged apprenticeships, even appealing to state supreme courts, and their descendants to help ascertain the intergenerational effect of these experiences and their effect on the persistence of America's racial inequality. While these cases tell their individual stories, the fates of their descendants tell our collective American story.

For all the contemporary terms we use to analyze white supremacy, and the century and a half of demands made by black people for ex-slave pensions and reparations, we don't have many stories about individual families. This book offers some of those missing narratives. What if these newly emancipated black people had been able to control their labor and earn just wages? What if they had been able to reunite their kinship networks and secure generational bonds? What if they had attained property and kept it? What if these black people were permitted to pursue the American Dream?

CHAPTER 1

THE LOST CHILDREN OF NATHAN AND JENNEY COX

Nathan and Jenney Cox did not understand why their children were taken from them. Nor did they understand why their efforts to retrieve them had failed. The Union won the war, but after Abraham Lincoln's assassination, ex-Confederates gained control of Alabama's government. Democrats maintained controls through violence and a lock on the courts. For the Coxes, in Russell County, Alabama, this political upheaval meant their pleas were rejected.

After the Thirteenth Amendment ended slavery, on December 6, 1865, the Cox parents' former master, Francis Jones (1824–1878), like many other slave owners acted quickly to try to keep his unpaid laborers as long as possible. Jones had owned seventy-five slaves, in the 1860 slave schedule of the US Census, $8,000 in real estate and $80,000 in personal property. This was at a time when most slaveholders owned less than ten slaves and the largest slaveholders had about 250 slaves.

Jones included the five Cox children—Nathan F. (Felix), age sixteen; Henry, age ten; Daniel, age six; Isham, age five; and Matt, age three—among twelve of the former slaves he persuaded the local probate judge to apprentice to him. On December 27,

1865, the Russell County probate court gave Jones an order indenturing the seven boys and five girls, including the Cox children, to him. The children were ordered into service up to age eighteen for girls and twenty-one for boys under the apprenticeship laws.[1]

In his application to the court, Jones was careful to attest to the requirements of the apprenticeship law by asserting that Nathan and Jenney were notified of his application for indentures and that the children were "young and inexperienced" and had "no means on which to support themselves, and that their parents are unable to provide a support for them." The children could not support "themselves without the assistance of some white person of experience." Further, unless they were apprenticed, they would "become an expense to the public community, or the county."[2]

Seven of the other children Jones procured—George, Marg, Anderson, Augustus, Jane, Alex, and an unnamed infant boy—had belonged to a man named George Washington. According to court records, he had been notified about the procurement but "refused" to attend the hearing. The only black George Washington in the vicinity was born in 1853 and married Lucy Whitsell on December 25, 1894, in Sumter, Alabama. He lived in Boligee, Greene County, in 1920, when he was sixty-nine, and rented a farm property.

Continuing President Lincoln's policy of implementing new governments in the states that had seceded, his successor, President Johnson, implemented a plan of Presidential Reconstruction. He appointed a provisional governor for Alabama in June 1865. Thereafter, a state convention met in September, voided the secession ordinance, and abolished slavery. A legislature and governor were elected in November, but the legislature's passage of Black Codes to control the freedmen, and its rejection of the Fourteenth Amendment, eventually led, as it did in the other ex-Confederate states, to Military Reconstruction, in 1867.

Jones's application to indenture the Cox children was handled by probate judge James Fleming Waddell, a local lawyer who was probably well-acquainted with Jones and other slave owners. He was a staunch supporter of and a military leader for the Confederacy. Waddell unsurprisingly decided that Jones had fully complied with the procedure outlined in the apprenticeship code. He found that the Coxes, who had appeared in court, could not receive custody of their children because they had "failed to prove their ability to support and provide for said minors."[3]

Though the Cox parents lost, they had reason to hope. Alabama was under Republican military rule until official restoration to the Union in 1868. Nathan Cox had registered to vote when the Republicans in 1867 gave black men, but not women, voting rights. The state legislature created a public school system for the first time and expanded women's property rights. Legislators funded numerous public road and railroad projects, although the ex-Confederate opponents claimed they engaged in fraud and misappropriation. However, organized resistance groups acted to suppress freedmen and Republicans. Although the Ku Klux Klan is the most well-known, also among these groups were the Knights of the White Camelia, Red Shirts, and White League.[4]

Freedmen's Bureau records show that the Cox parents kept trying to regain their children. With the bureau's help, Nathan Cox appealed the decision to the state supreme court asking that the order be reversed because he and Jenney had not been notified and could care for their children. But Judge William McKendree Byrd's opinion for the court deciding against him cited convoluted procedural grounds for the ruling.[5]

Byrd (1817–1874), the son of William H. Byrd of Richland, Mississippi, was born on December 6, 1817, in Perry County, Mississippi. He attended La Grange College and, after graduation, settled in Holly Springs, Mississippi. He later moved to Linden, Alabama, where he began the practice of law and became prominent in the political life of his state starting with election, in 1851, to the state legislature. Byrd was elected as an associate justice by the ex-Confederate-controlled legislature on January 2, 1866. When Republicans gained control, he was removed in 1868 under the Military Reconstruction Constitution.

Judge Byrd was unsympathetic to the complaint of the Cox parents. In upholding the indentures of their children, Byrd chose not to focus on false imprisonment or on the absence of evidence showing the notification of the parents. He interpreted the law as relying on the discretion of the probate judge and including no mechanism for direct appeal. Cox could have filed a writ of habeas corpus as a matter of due process if he'd had the resources to do so, but Judge Byrd's opinion made clear Cox would likely have lost regardless.

After their parents, Nathan and Jenney Cox, lost their children to their former master, Francis Jones, the children eventually took the name Jones. Nathan and Jenney, however, like other freed people, left the Jones plantation when the politics changed and former slave owners pretended apprenticeships were no longer feasible. Continued violence and intimidation remained threats as ex-Confederates insisted on regaining control of the state. At great risk, black men could vote, as Nathan did, starting in 1867 when Congress enacted Military Reconstruction, and the Freedmen's Bureau was at least a presence in the area, from its founding in 1865 to its ending in 1872.

By 1870, Nathan Jones was living in York, Sumter County, Alabama, and he rented a home and farmed; his son Rolly, seventeen, farmed with him. Matt, Daniel, and Isham, using the Jones last name, lived with Henry in Russell County, Alabama, in 1880, when he would have been age twenty-five, both working as farmhands. Henry still lived in the county as a farmer with a mortgage on his home in 1890. His children became farm laborers who, by the third generation, could read and write. Matt Jones, in 1920, worked as a quarryman in a stone mill and lived with his wife, Lizzie, and her parents in Russellville, Franklin County, Alabama. In 1930 he was still a quarryman in a stone mill, and in 1940, at age seventy-seven, he lived with Lizzie in Russellville and worked as laborer and lived in a house they rented. He had no schooling. Though Jones descendants of Nathan and Jenny Cox stayed in Alabama, and kept some family ties, the fate of Nathan and Jenny Cox and any descendants remains unclear. The inexplicable loss of their children had a lasting effect. Like those of most of the formerly enslaved and their descendants, their experiences limited the ability to gain social and economic opportunity. Demoralized and poor, they tried to make the best of their freedom.

CHAPTER 2

FREEING HENRY COMAS

Jacob, a free man of color, while a slave on the Comas's Appling, Georgia, plantation, established a conjugal relationship with a neighboring slave woman, Easter, with the consent of both their owners. During five years, they had five children, including Henry, born in about 1851. Jacob Comas ended the relationship with Easter and established a new relationship with another woman, which was not unusual during slavery. Sometime, thereafter, Easter died. Upon the death of his mother, Henry automatically became the slave of his mother's owner, Isham Reddish.

Reddish (1812–1889) lived with his wife and six children in Appling County on a prosperous plantation. In 1850, he had only four slaves: two eighteen-year-olds, one male and one female; and a female, age fifteen; and one female, one month old. By 1860 he had twenty-six, including Henry Comas, who lived among four slave cabins and real estate worth $2,000 and a personal estate of $1,900.[1]

Jacob Comas had been a slave of John Comas, who had left Spain in 1822, spent time in New Orleans and Baltimore, and then landed in Georgia and eventually ran a river flatboat. John then settled in Appling County. The area's early economic activity consisted primarily of small-scale subsistence farming until

sales of livestock, timber, and naval stores to Savannah and elsewhere grew. Cotton became important in the 1860s before the
Civil War. The county was named in posthumous honor for Colonel Daniel Appling, a well-known hero of the War of 1812. The
original county consisted of lands from which the Creeks were
expelled during and after the Creek Indian War of 1813–1814.

By 1860, John Comas had prospered. His real estate was
valued at $500 and personal property at $17,490, and he owned
seventeen slaves. They included a male and female, both age
fifty; a male, age thirty-five; a male and female, both age thirty;
and the others ranging from one nineteen-year-old woman and
younger males and females. The youngest child was a female,
age eighteen months.

Henry Comas stayed at Reddish's place until about September 1865, when he left and went to Jacob Comas, who had also
prospered, "claiming and recognizing him as his father."[2] He
stayed with him in Appling County, where his father "kept and
maintained him." Isham Reddish admitted, even as he tried to
keep Henry, that Jacob was "a man of good character for honesty
industry and morality—that he has a good crop as any man white
or black in the neighborhood the present years and that he is
abundantly able to provide for support and maintain his family."

During the Civil War, not much military activity took place
in Appling County, though able-bodied men from the community joined the Confederate service. General William Tecumseh
Sherman's 1864 march through Georgia devastated large areas
but left Savannah, the closest commercial center for Appling
County, largely untouched. John Comas served in the Confederate infantry as a private for about three months in 1862 and
was then assigned to help gather "conscripts." After the war, he
became a very successful merchandiser, purchasing a general
store in Baxley, the county seat of Wayne, in 1878. He retired in

1884 and died in 1895, leaving the merchandising business to his heirs, who continued it. Isham Reddish fought as a corporal in the Twenty-Fourth Regiment, Company E, for the South Carolina Infantry. Drew Reddish, the oldest of Isham's sons, born in 1845, served in the Georgia Militia.

The case, *Comas v. Reddish*, in which Isham defeated Jacob Comas, arose after the devastation of the Confederate defeat and the end of legal slavery, in December 1865. Isham Reddish decided, like other former slaveholders, who resented the South's defeat and the area's overall economic distress, that he wanted Henry to return to work for him for free, as he had during slavery. In March 1866, under Presidential Reconstruction, Georgia, like other Southern states, passed new apprenticeship legislation amending the laws concerning apprentices. The new law was ostensibly designed to provide for the large number of "colored minors" who, because of the Civil War, were "thrown upon society, helpless from want of parental protection, want of means of support, inability to earn their daily bread, and from age and other causes."[3] In fact, it was designed to help the planters who wanted to keep black children as unpaid labor as long as possible.

During Andrew Johnson's plan of Reconstruction, under which many ex-Confederates were still in the state government including the judiciary, the county probate judge, called the Ordinary, without notifying Henry or his father, Jacob Comas, in May 1866 approved Reddish's request that he apprentice Henry to him. The Ordinary "recited," as the grounds of his approval, despite Isham Reddish's admission to the contrary, that it seemed Henry "was without any parent residing in that county, and without means for his support and education."[4]

Henry, in fact, was living with his father, Jacob Comas, in the county, which Reddish knew when he filed the writ of habeas corpus demanding his return. Reddish's actions amounted to trafficking Henry. At the superior court trial, Henry testified that he wanted to stay with his father who "left it optional with him either to remain with him or to return to his former slave owner." Henry said he remained "of his own free will because he thought he was as much entitled to freedom as others."[5] John Comas testified that he knew that Jacob and Easter, Henry's mother, claimed a husband-and-wife relationship though he never knew they were married.

The color question carried weight when Freedmen's Bureau officials decided whether to help a former slave woman who claimed someone was her husband and father of her children based on whether the children were lighter colored than the soldier identified. For example, after Union troops expelled Confederate control, a soldier in Nashville, Tennessee, in August 1865 wanted his wife back in Clarksville to join him. The woman wouldn't leave their daughter, whom the plantation owner wanted to keep enslaved. The Freedmen's Bureau agent gave her an order for their daughter's release. The slave owner complied, but when mother and daughter started down the road, he beat the mother "with a club and left her senseless on the ground after which he returned home with the child."[6] The slave owner was arrested by the Freedmen's Bureau and fined $100 for maltreating the mother, but meanwhile the soldier had given up and "married" another woman. Bureau officials refused to dissolve the new "marriage," because upon seeing that some of the children of his original wife were "mulattoes" and others "black," they did not believe, based on the soldier's color, that he could have fathered them all. The mother was treated as a loose woman who could not be helped.[7]

In *Comas v. Reddish*, the color question in the lower court had a similarly negative effect on Jacob Comas's case. When asked if he thought Henry was too light colored to be Jacob's son, John Comas explained that "he could not tell that a black bull sometimes was the father of a white or light calf, that defendant was very black." But one plaintiff's witness, E. D. Graham had a certain conclusion. His testimony was "in his opinion the boy Henry was too light colored to be begotten by defendant, he being a very black man."[8]

Judge W. M. Sessions held that since the indentures of apprenticeship were executed by the Ordinary, a court of competent jurisdiction, he could not set them aside and awarded Henry to Reddish.[9]

In June 1866, the Fourteenth Amendment was enacted by Congress, but the Georgia legislature refused to ratify it, only adding to the impetus for Republicans in Congress to enact Military Reconstruction. These developments were critical when Jacob Comas appealed to the Supreme Court of Georgia. The court reversed Sessions's ruling in December 1866.

Supreme court judge Iverson Louis Harris returned Henry to his father, citing the March 1866 apprenticeship law, passed by the Georgia legislature to effectively re-enslave African American minors. Harris called the law as "wise, just, and humane, and comprehends, alike, the white and black, without discrimination."[10] It required that public officials should "be vigilant in preventing any one, under the name of master, from getting the control of the labor and services of such minor apprentice, as if he were still a slave. It should be borne always in mind, and at all times should regulate the conduct of the white man, that slavery is with the days beyond the flood," being prohibited by the constitution of the State of Georgia and the Thirteenth Amendment. Therefore "its continuance will not by any honest public functionary be tolerated, under the forms of law or otherwise, directly or indirectly."[11]

The 1866 Apprenticeship Act did not "envision indenturing a colored minor in this kind of case." When the parents are dead and the "profits or income of their estate are insufficient for the support of the minor," then the Ordinary could bind out the minor. Specifically, the law provides that in all cases where the parents are, from poverty, infirmity, from disease or old age, unable to support their minor children, the Ordinary is authorized to bind out their children.

Harris concluded that the Ordinary had no jurisdiction in the case, and the testimony included "the strongest reasons why he should not have yielded to the wish of Reddish to have the boy Henry apprenticed to him."[12]

While Henry Comas and his relatives lived the kind of working-class existence common for blacks coming from slavery, employed in domestic service and laboring, the Reddishes remained fairly prosperous and passed along their status intergenerationally. Though they suffered some losses with the end of slavery, Isham and his descendants continued to hold property and make a living from farming using farmhands. We don't know, however, what they paid them.

The descendants of Jacob Comas may not have known the story of how he managed to free himself and then Henry, and to move away from the Reddish slave owners, but they quickly joined the flow of migrants to Florida. During the Civil War, Gainesville had been a Confederate supply depot and the site of two battles. When abolition came, large numbers of migrants from Southern states that were more devastated by the war migrated from Georgia, South Carolina, and Alabama. Many went to Florida for its climate and to Alachua County in particular for its farming of fruits, vegetables, and sea island cotton and relatively easy freight-train transportation from Gainesville, which became the Alachua County seat.

For several months following the Civil War, the Third United States Colored Troops were stationed in Gainesville, which encouraged freed men to settle there. At the same time, black farm laborers were recruited from Georgia and South Carolina to help harvest what was expected to be a very large cotton crop, but heavy rain ruined the cotton and work for the new black migrants. The black population still increased, and black segregated and businesses grew in Gainesville. Under Republican Reconstruction, the immigration of freed slaves and economic growth meant that when the ex-Confederates took over, the Alachua County population had grown, and Gainesville was a growing mercantile center for cotton and vegetable crops. Although severe freezes occasionally created problems, by the twentieth century Alachua County had a growing economy with a base including the phosphate, cotton, vegetable, and citrus industries.

Florida's first black congressman, Josiah T. Walls (1842–1905), who lived in Alachua County, served from 1871 to 1876. He was the only black member of Congress from Florida until the 1990s, when Carrie Meek (1926–2021) and Alcee Hastings (1936–2021) were elected. The state's election laws of 1889 almost completely disenfranchised black voters, and "Jim Crow" laws were enacted.

The Comases' slavery experiences, like those of other blacks, formed a significant part of their history and limitations on their prospects. After the Supreme Court of Georgia decision, there are some clues to what happened to Jacob and his descendants. In the first generation, they, not surprisingly, were farmers and domestic laborers. By 1870, Jane and Jacob Comas lived with their five children in Alachua County, Florida. They were all reported in the US Census as having been born in Georgia; Jane was keeping house, and father and children were farming.[13]

After his apprenticeship to Reddish was dissolved, by 1910, Henry Comas, who left his father Jacob's household by 1870, when he was twenty, lived in Bibb County, Georgia, with his wife, Jincey. They were married for forty years, from 1870. Henry worked as a coachman, and she as a laundress, both for a private family. Henry owned their property free and clear and could read and write.[14]

In 1880, Jacob and Jane Comas still lived in Alachua County, Florida. By that time, only a grandson, Jacob, age five, and a granddaughter, Jane, age seven, lived with them. Jacob died in Alachua County in 1930. None of the Comas family members ever were reported in the census as attending school. Jacob and Jane's grandson registered for the World War I draft in 1918, at age forty-five.[15]

In 1920, when Jacob Sr., who won the apprenticeship case gaining custody of his son, Henry, died, his grandson Jacob (Jake), forty-four, who was single and could read and write though not having attended school, and his grandmother, the widow, Jane, lived on a farm Jake owned. The farm, in Orange Heights, Alachua County, Florida, had no outstanding mortgage and specialized in growing vegetables.

During the early twentieth century, the boll weevil decimated Alachua's cotton, and World War I undermined the phosphate industry. But the University of Florida, established in Gainesville in 1905, by 1930 was the most important driver of the economy, helping to relieve the effects of the Great Depression.

In 1930, grandson Jake Comas lived alone. He still owned a farm but reported to the US Census no specialty, just general farming. Also in 1930, Eliza Reddish, who was a black fifty-one- or fifty-four-year-old widow, born in Georgia, lived alone next to Jacob and worked as a laundress. She, like the black Comas family, did not attend school but could read and write. She died on June 26, 1954, at age seventy-nine in Glynn, Georgia.[16] In 1870, Eliza, "mulatto," the youngest of four children, and her black mother, Ila, twenty-eight, and her father, Moton Reddish, a "mulatto" farmer, age forty-five, could have been on the Isham Reddish plantation during slavery.

CHAPTER 3

THE RESCUE OF MARY CANNON

The other formerly enslaved people who won, or lost, the state supreme court reported apprenticeship cases did not manage to become educated or middle class. However, they, for the most part, managed to become self-sufficient as working-class farmers, factory workers, or domestic employees.

Six-year-old Mary Cannon found herself "apprenticed" by her former owner to a neighboring white farmer, James Stuart, without her parents' permission in 1866. Mary's parents' marriage during their enslavement was not legally recognized, so they could not sue to regain custody, and Mary was too young to sue on her own behalf. Julia Cannon, a white woman, took up Mary's cause and brought the case as a "next friend," an adult who represents an underage person.[1]

Mary's family—her parents, James, born in 1847, and Emeline, born in 1845, and her siblings—had been enslaved by Elisha Cannon in Dagsboro, Sussex County, Delaware, before the Civil War. Dagsboro, incorporated in the early 1900s, is today a small town about fifteen miles from Rehoboth Beach. Its history can be dated to at least 1630, when Blackfoot Indians migrated south from New Jersey and settled on a tributary of a large body of water known then as Indian River. The village was called Blackfoot

Town, and as English settlers found their way to the area and the Blackfoot gradually were moved near the Nanticoke River, the settlement retained its name. In 1774, William Penn granted a tract of land that included Blackfoot Town to General John Dagworthy, who fought in the Revolutionary War. The name of Blackfoot Town, changed to Dagsborough in honor of the general, by 1747 became Dagsboro.[2]

The early antebellum local economy based on plantation agriculture—corn, wheat, and foodstuffs—cypress timberland and sawmills, and the enslaved labor of slaves, produced the wealth of plantation owners. After the Revolution, wheat, which required less labor, soon replaced corn and tobacco as cash crops.[3]

Why did a member of a slaveholding family intervene in the apprenticing of Mary Cannon? Julia Cannon's personal family history likely influenced her actions. Her parents, Samuel and Elizabeth Messick, were probably antislavery Methodists. Records show they either owned no slaves at all or at one point possibly owned a slave, who lived at their house. The freeing of slaves, by manumission often in the owner's will, increased in Delaware as elsewhere in the North after the Revolutionary War, as the Quakers, who were a dominant force in the northern end of the state, near Philadelphia, turned firmly against slave owning. The Methodists gained numbers in the state's southern end. And, yet, there was a failed attempt to abolish slavery in the new state constitution of Pennsylvania in 1792.

Thereafter, bills to abolish slavery were introduced in the General Assembly, even after the Speaker of the state House of Representatives killed an 1803 gradual emancipation effort by casting the tiebreaking vote. However, the pattern of antislavery New Castle County in the northern part of the state and proslavery Sussex County in the south became entrenched. In the years after Julia's father Samuel Messick's 1842 death, abolition legislation introduced in the legislature continued to fail.[4]

After Julia Messick married into the family of Mary's owner, Elisha Cannon, in 1856, she and her husband, John C. Cannon, continued to live downstate. In 1860, their child, Sarah E., and a servant, a farmer's apprentice, and two young relatives lived with them. They had no slaves. John Cannon and Elisha Cannon, who had somehow lost sight in one eye, all registered for the national government's first draft in June 1863. Elisha was thirty-nine and still single. John served in Company B, Sixth Delaware Infantry, during the war.[5]

Delaware prides itself on being "The First State" in ratifying the US Constitution, but it was among the last to ratify the Thirteenth Amendment outlawing slavery, waiting until February 1901, more than thirty-five years after the end of the Civil War, when the amendment had been ratified by three-fourths of the states and was already in effect.

When Julia, in 1866, filed a habeas corpus plea for Mary Cannon's release, her actions also seemed compatible with John Cannon's service in the Union Army and her parents' nonparticipation in the plantation way of life. Whatever Elisha Cannon's views, Julia apparently disapproved of the tactic of re-enslaving black children through apprenticeship, which was widespread when abolition took place at the end of the Civil War.[6]

James Stuart, the neighboring planter who had indentured Mary, apparently so sure of prevailing that he waived a hearing and submitted the case for decision by the Delaware Superior Court, lost in an opinion to John Wallace Houston, a lawyer and politician from Georgetown, in Sussex County. Houston was a member of the Whig Party and the Democratic Party, and he also served as a US representative from Delaware. Houston was born on May 4, 1814, in Concord, Delaware, attended the county schools and Newark Academy, and graduated from Yale in 1834. He moved to Georgetown, Delaware, in 1839 and began a law practice. He had been a slaveholder.

Houston was secretary of state of Delaware from 1841 to 1844 and was elected, as a Whig, to the Twenty-Ninth, Thirtieth, and Thirty-First Congresses, serving from March 4, 1845, to March 3, 1851. While in the House, he was chairman of the Committee on Public Buildings and Grounds for the Thirtieth Congress. He was not a candidate for renomination in 1850 and was appointed associate judge of the Delaware Superior Court on May 4, 1855, serving until his retirement in 1893. He was a member of the Peace Conference of 1861, held in Washington, DC, in an effort to prevent the Civil War.[7]

In Mary Cannon's case, Houston pointed out that certainly a state law provided that a "negro or mulatto child bound . . . has no remedy by petition to be discharged except for cruelty, ill-usage, treatment not conformable to the terms of binding and breach of contract." The nonconsensual apprenticing of a six-year-old child in itself did not constitute "cruelty" or "ill-usage." However, Judge Houston found this concern too narrow. Mary could be released from the apprenticeship for any procedural "illegality or invalidity whatever in the binding for habeas corpus is a constitutional protection whatever is done statutorily."[8]

Based on the facts, the constable in the case who gave evidence used by the two justices of the peace to bind Mary did not follow correct procedures necessary for a valid apprenticeship to exist. He gave no notice, much less thirty days' notice, to her mother, which the law required. He ignored the requirement to give her mother an opportunity to provide "a suitable home for her with some respectable white person in the mean while." Also, "the justices of the peace bound her without delaying until the required five days after their hearing of the case, to give her mother a chance to indemnify the county so there was no danger of Mary becoming a charge upon the state." The court found the procedures used were illegal, thus supporting the use of the state constitutional habeas corpus remedy to free Mary from the apprenticeship. Largely the manner of her "capture" rather than the issues raised by the apprenticeship system formed the basis of the decision.[9]

After the case was decided, there is no record of contact between the black Cannons and the whites. Julia's family and descendants like the black Cannons led working-class lives thereafter. Julia and John Cannon had six children, but only one Phillip Barr (1862–1932) lived past age eighteen. He died from myocarditis and arteriosclerosis. Julia was widowed in 1880 and filed for her husband's military pension on May 15, 1882. She died in 1912.[10]

Over the years, as Mary and her siblings matured, their former slave owner who had tried to apprentice her, Elisha Cannon, continued to be active in the political and business communities. He was on the Dagsboro Republican ticket for state representative in 1870. He was also a director of the Breakwater and Frankford Railroad Company.[11]

The black Cannons continued to live on the Cannon plantation for a few years after Mary escaped the apprenticeship, which was not unusual for the newly freed formerly enslaved. In the first US census after Mary's 1867 case, in 1870, her parents, James Cannon, a farm laborer, age twenty-three, and Emmeline, a servant, age twenty-five, still lived with their children—Mary, age eight, and her three siblings, Francis, age ten; Joshua, six;

and Charles, one—on Elisha W. Cannon's property.[12] James and Emmaline's children remained uneducated at first. In 1865, there were only seven schools in the state for blacks, though Delaware had 1,798 slaves and 9,829 free negroes in 1860. Blacks sought advice from Marylanders who had organized to gain education for free Negroes as their religious leaders, Methodists and Quakers, pressed the state to have schools for blacks, calling themselves the Delaware Association for the Moral Improvement of Colored People. They achieved the right to levy taxes for schools in their districts but failed to collect what the state expected in 1892. By 1897, the state constitution had created segregated public schools under control of state.

In 1880, formerly enslaved Mary Cannon, age eighteen, and her siblings, Prince, age twenty, who was not listed in the 1870 US Census; Joshua, age fourteen; Bell, age nine; and Horace, age six, along with James and Emmaline, resided within the Cannon domain. The black Cannons, even the youngest ones, remained servants, still living on Elisha Cannon's property.[13]

A major change in the family occurred after December 1883, when Mary H. Cannon married farm laborer John T. Vickers, the son of Nathaniel Vickers and Fannie Burton, in Sussex. Because the 1890 US Census was completely burned, it is unclear when, but by 1900, Mary and John had moved with their children to a rented house in Sussex while he continued his employment as a farm laborer. Seven of their children were born between 1880 and 1897.[14] By 1910, Joshua, age twenty-five, and Ernest, nineteen, were still with their parents, along with five of the younger children: Howard, Cutie, Willis, Kate, and Edmunce. Minnie, who would have been twenty-three; John, who would have been seventeen; and Gertrude, who would have been thirteen, were no longer in the household. John Vickers was still farming on a rented property.[15]

According to land records, John and Mary Vickers sold thirteen and a half acres of land to their children, Joshua, Ernest,
and Howard, in 1917 for $650. Also, John's brother George sold
his thirteen and a half acres of the same parcel to his nephews
in 1918 for $675. George's and John's acreages had been willed
to them from their mother, Fannie T. Burton Vickers, who purchased thirty acres of land from William and Ella Short on January 13, 1891. Fannie Vickers died in 1899.[16]

On September 7, 1917, Howard Vickers was among the men
called to appear at the county draft board in Georgetown to
determine their fitness for World War I military service. On
October 4, 1917, the local press reported that he was one of
thirty-nine men rejected by the Sussex board because they failed
to pass the physical. Eighteen men were approved for service.[17]

By 1920, Mary and John Vickers had another daughter, fourteen-
year-old Elsie, making a total of eleven children. Six of their
children and two granddaughters, Mary Hall and Delia Hall,
lived with them. Mary Cannon Vickers died June 17, 1923, and
John T. Vickers died April 3, 1929, both in, Sussex, Delaware.[18]

After *Cannon v. Stuart* freed Mary Cannon from the apprenticeship, the black Cannons and descendants remained
working-class people, laboring on farms or in service occupations after Emancipation. After Mary married John Vickers, the
second generation inherited some property from Vickers parents
and were able to hold on to some of it. Also, by the second
generation and thereafter, they usually had a primary school
education, at least through the fourth grade. Of those eligible
registered for the draft when war came, none had criminal records noted and were generally hard-working people. They then
rented or tried to save to buy farm property. Thereafter, into the
late twentieth century, the black Cannons mostly stayed close
to each other in Delaware and in Pennsylvania and maintained

family ties. A few were institutionalized as suffering from mental illness. When they died, most had suffered from cardiac disease, hypertension, diabetes, tuberculosis, and possibly cancer. They rarely lived beyond their fifties or sixties. The black Cannons' economic and racial distress originated in slavery, discrimination, and segregation, effects of which remain today.

CHAPTER 4

THE EMANCIPATION OF ELIZA AND HARRIET AMBROSE

H epsey Saunders, a former slave, gave birth to her children, Harriet and Eliza and John Allen, during slavery. Not unusual at the time, given deaths, runaways, and the forced inability to maintain families, they each had different fathers. When slavery was abolished, in 1865, Hepsey's former slave owner refused to let her take the children, keeping them as supposed apprentices. Hepsey received a positive response when she came to the Freedmen's Bureau for help. The bureau decided the support of Hepsey's new legal husband, freedman Wiley Ambrose, might increase the odds of success in the legal system. Eventually, the Ambrose parents regained her children. Their victory in the North Carolina Supreme Court also made new law by creating a legal theory that benefited other parents seeking to retrieve their children.[1]

Winning the case was in part attributable to Hepsey Saunders's marriage to Wiley Ambrose, as he legally assumed the responsibilities of husband and stepfather. Nonetheless, in December 1865, her former owner, Daniel Russell, convinced the Robeson County Court to bind her three children to him, ignoring the mother and stepfather's parental rights. The 1860

US Census slave schedule of the county fourteen miles below Wilmington and across the Cape Fear River in North Carolina includes slaves of an age and gender who fit Eliza and Harriet and their mother, Hepsey.

The Ambrose parents had a formidable opponent in their fight. Daniel Lindsay Russell Sr. was also a North Carolina justice of the peace, serving in Brunswick County, and easily got the Robeson County court's approval for his apprenticeship of at least twenty formerly enslaved children, including Eliza and Harriet Ambrose. The Russells markedly managed to manipulate formerly enslaved men's votes for political power during Reconstruction, and Daniel Jr. was elected governor in 1894. However, their immediate post–Civil War problem, like that of other former slave owners, was how to maintain free labor in a time of economic depression with slavery ended. Apprenticing formerly enslaved children seemed a convenient source for the workers they needed.

Moreover, in this matter, Russell was willing to defy the Freedmen's Bureau's dictates as he continued to "apprentice" stolen children. The Russells had long been a power in the county. Daniel Russell had moved from Onslow County to Brunswick County in about 1820. By the early 1800s, he had developed the property once owned by acting British governor Nathaniel Rice before the Revolution into a 28,000-acre plantation with more than two hundred slaves on nearby Town Creek. He had become a Whig in the 1830s as leaders such as Henry Clay organized to oppose Andrew Jackson. His service for many years as the presiding magistrate of the justice of the peace courts of Brunswick County reflected his social position locally and aided his ability to manipulate apprenticeship law. He held the judicial position until the abolition of the court in 1868 during Reconstruction.

Exploiting North Carolina's pine forests, Russell's plantations produced naval stores of turpentine, rosin, and tar, for which Wilmington had become a major export capital, and cotton instead of rice. In the 1840s, Russell built a new house close by, using doorknobs, doors, hinges, and some building materials from the old house, in which his son Daniel Jr., the future North Carolina governor (from 1897 to 1901) was born, in 1845.[2]

Russell, like many white North Carolinians, including committed Whigs, opposed secession until after the firing on Fort Sumter and President Lincoln's call for troops to suppress the rebellion. The abolition of slavery decimated the slaveholder economy, leaving Russell and other planters bereft of labor.

Wiley Ambrose had his own experiences and reputation to buttress a claim to Harriet and Eliza. He was probably one of the formerly enslaved men in the Union forces who fought in the strategic battles in the area. During the war, the Confederacy relied heavily on the Wilmington port for imports of clothing, food, and weaponry exchanged for cotton and tobacco. British smugglers ran the union blockade, sometimes using Confederate insignia since the Union put to death British pirates captured in the trading.

After the Union took Norfolk, in May 1862, Fort Fisher, fifteen miles south of the port, provided Wilmington with strong Confederate defenses until the war's conclusion. Many black troops fought and died, along with white regiments, in the final months of the war as part of the Union capture of Fort Fisher. As the war concluded, some survivors were mustered out and stayed in the area. Thousands of Union soldiers who died in the assault on Fort Fisher and the Wilmington campaign were reburied in unmarked graves in the cemetery when it opened in 1867. Wiley Ambrose was probably one of the surviving soldiers.

Presenting herself and her husband as a "well to do" couple with "good character," Hepsey Saunders asked the Freedmen's Bureau in the summer of 1866 for help in regaining Harriet, age thirteen, and Eliza, fifteen, from Russell.[3] After the bureau gave her an order permitting her to retrieve them, she showed it at Russell's place and took the children home. But in September of that year, Russell took Hepsey's children again, having easily obtained apprenticeships from the county court despite having been ordered to stop taking the children. Persisting, Hepsey and Wiley went to Russell's place again in December 1866 to reclaim her children. Russell drove them away, threating arrest if they proceeded.[4]

With black parents begging the Freedmen's Bureau to help them regain their children, Assistant Commissioner John Robinson threatened to cancel the indentures as an abuse of law. By October 1866, he concluded that Russell took children who had resided with capable parents, essentially kidnapping them using the apprenticeship law. Robinson told Governor Jonathan Worth, "It looks to me like the reestablishment of slavery under the mild name of apprenticeship."

Freedmen's Bureau officials in the central office, considering Russell a "designing and unscrupulous man" intent on restoring slavery in all but name, canceled the indentures he had received and ordered Harriet and Eliza returned to their parents. Russell ignored them and continued to hold the children. Assistant Commissioner Robinson, with the full support of Commissioner Oliver O. Howard, decided to make an example of Russell by challenging the indentures and the state's apprenticeship laws and practices as a violation of the Civil Rights Act of 1866. The act, based on the Thirteenth Amendment, forbade discrimination on the basis of the previous condition of servitude in the making of contracts. Blacks would only need to show that the terms offered to blacks were more burdensome than those required of whites and amounted to discrimination. They needed also to prove the ability to support their children to nullify the indenture to Russell.

The bureau lawyers decided it was more practical to seek a court order to subdue Russell using the Ambrose case instead of pursuing Lucy Ross's claims for the return of her children. They reached this conclusion despite Lucy's ability to care for her daughters, Maria and Delia, ages sixteen and twelve. Her two brothers confirmed that she remained "fully able and willing to support" her children, and a neighbor testified Lucy could support her children from her work in the fields.[5] The local agent, in requesting to cancel the indentures, told his superior officers that they "were both earning wages" and that Maria was, in fact, "a grown woman." Further nothing undermined Lucy's insistence that she "never gave any consent" to have them apprenticed.

The Freedmen's Bureau lawyers chose the case of Eliza and Harriet's mother, Hepsey Saunders, and their stepfather, Wiley Ambrose, with Ambrose as their petitioner because Lucy was a single mother. She lived without being dependent on a man, and the North Carolina apprenticeship law permitted courts to bind out any child "not living with fathers." The legal argument they saw as much more likely to win in court avoided challenging gender distinctions and relied on a defense of formerly enslaved black fathers' rights as parents and citizens.[6]

Therefore, *In the Matter of Harriet Ambrose and Eliza Ambrose*, in the North Carolina Supreme Court in January 1867, was described as the illegal indentures of Ambrose's stepdaughters. The lawyers insisted that Harriet and Eliza resided in Wiley's free and independent black household. Further, the lower court that issued the indentures violated habeas corpus in that neither Wiley nor the children were notified of the indenture proceedings.[7]

Associate Justice Edwin Godwin Reade heard the bureau's legal arguments but chose to rely on his own experience and previous cases in his court about domesticity and the rights of the children to void the indentures. He, who had been a slaveholder but was a Unionist and a Republican elected a justice of the state supreme court, pointed out that Harriet and Eliza were "industrious well-behaved" young women who had been "amply provided for in food and clothing." They also, Reade noted, lived "with their mother and step-father," who possessed "good character" and were "well to do." "What better off could they be, or need they be," he asked and continued: "What interest had society in having their relations broken up, and themselves put under the care of strangers, with no affection for them, nor any other interest, except gain from their services."

Reade insisted on "a high duty" of the courts to turn to apprenticeship only "to protect . . . helpless children, and not only to prevent oppression and fraud, but to act as friends and guardians, and improve their condition." Before an indenture is ordered, the children as well as "their parents or friends who have charge of them" should be in the courtroom so as to "hear their own simple story." He concluded that, had the children been present and heard from, the court would never have seen a reason to apprentice Ambrose's children. The formerly enslaved girls "were entitled to notice before they could be bound out, and, as they had no notice, and were not present, the binding was void." At "an age" when they were "most in need of the oversight of their parents and friends," the girls had been subjected to a "a gross outrage."

However he arrived at his ruling in *Ambrose*, the Freedmen's Bureau saw a great victory for the rights of formerly enslaved parents and children. The court decision is known for its requirement of parental consent before an indenture constituting apprenticeship could be granted in the state. This ruling helped to limit efforts to steal formerly enslaved children in North Carolina.

Before the *Ambrose* decision, the law permitted approval of indentures without parental permission. A judge needed only to find custodial parents unsuitable to maintain and educate their children. This view would continue for decades, influencing child custody and foster care dispositions. Also, the state could legally apprentice any child who was born out of wedlock. This definition, of course, included anyone born a slave since slaves could not marry legally.[8]

The bureau interpreted the law as now requiring not just knowledge that the children were taken but actual parental consent in indentures made for freedchildren. The decision "will operate to annul all cases of apprenticeship in the State, where the children have been bound out, against the will of their parents," insisted the acting assistant commissioner of the Freedmen's Bureau in North Carolina in February 1867.[9]

Freedmen's Bureau commissioner Howard told Congress in late 1867 that the Civil Rights Act and the nation's highest court promised "the liberation of hundreds of freed children wrested from parents who were too poor or too humble to battle successfully with unjust tribunals."[10] However, there was no consistent rule. Some Freedmen's Bureau agents allowed local courts to re-indenture apprentices with parental notification; other agents insisted on parental permission. The head of the bureau in North Carolina voided indentures where parents did not consent "in accordance with the recent decision of the Supreme Court of North Carolina in the Case of Ambrose v. Russel[l]."

Although the case was decided on narrow grounds, and the ruling did not end all child stealing, it was used to end many apprenticeships that had been created after the abolition of slavery in 1865. In May 1867, the Carteret, Middlesex County, New

Jersey, court canceled all indentures contrary to the court decision in Harriet and Eliza's case and announced it would not approve any others unless with the consent of the parents or next of kin and the appearance of the children in court.

After the *Ambrose* decision, courts continued to reject the claims of single mothers. In October 1867, Lucy Ross tried but failed to protect her daughters from Russell, who was back in court obtaining indentures for them and other children.[11]

Based on the procedural requirements of the *Ambrose* decision, Marina Mitchell of Hertford County, North Carolina, was able to protect her parental rights and keep her children—Alfred, Dick, Thomas, and Catherine—from the clutches of their slave owner, Miles Mitchell, in 1871. Miles Mitchell secured an approval of an indenture of the children from the Hertford County probate judge. With the aid of the Freedmen's Bureau, Marina filed a successful habeas corpus proceeding, and mother and children were served and ordered to appear at a hearing.

The record noted, "Upon the day set apart for the hearing, neither the mother nor the children were present, having been prevented from attending by the inclemency of the weather."[12] The probate judge proceeded without them and ordered the children turned over as apprentices to Miles Mitchell. Marina Mitchell appealed to the Superior Court, and the matter was heard in the fall term, 1871. The court found that Marina had made good financial decisions for herself and the children. She hired out the oldest child for the year, for $60. The youngest, Catherine, lived with a family whose head was a lawyer, "a respectable gentleman." The other two lived with her and helped to farm rented land, with a team of animals. They had made an average crop compared to others in the area. Marina was described as "industrious and frugal" and as taking "good care of her children, as colored mothers generally do. All of the children

together could have been hired out at $12.50 per month." Marina
would get directly half of everything raised, and she received a
horse and provisions that Miles sold to her; "at the end of the
year she would be in debt to . . . Mitchell about $100 for pro-
visions, which it would take the most of her part of the crop to
satisfy." The superior court finding, that "Miles Mitchell was a
kind and humane man, and in every respect a fit and suitable
person for a master of apprentices," upheld the indenturing of
Marina's children.

But Miles Mitchell lost in the state supreme court because
Chief Justice Reade and his colleagues had laid down the requirements that first the apprenticeship code must be followed and
that parents' concerns and rights were protected. Reade began,
"In ex parte Ambrose, 61 N.C. 91, it is said that notice to persons
to be bound out, or to their friends, is indispensable, and that it
is prudent to have them present in person before the Court."[13]
If they were prevented by the weather from being present, the
judge should have rescheduled the case until he could see them,
inspect them, and ascertain their needs; "also in order that the
public may see the children, so that there may be competition
among applicants for their services, as no one would like to take
an apprentice without seeing the person. There may be circumstances to excuse the binding in the absence of the children, but
none appears in this case."[14]

After the decision leaving Harriet and Eliza with their stepfather and mother, until his death in 1871, Russell kept trying
to gain apprentices and other workers to keep his plantation
afloat. In an effort to stay solvent and exercise some power,
during Reconstruction he and his son Daniel Jr. (eventual governor of North Carolina) became Republicans. Daniel Jr. won
election as a judge on the Republican ticket in 1868 with black,
carpetbagger, and scalawag white votes and served until 1874.

He wrote a strong opinion protecting black civil rights to public accommodations without discrimination. But the ex-Confederate takeover of the legislature led to his defeat for a second term. Ironically, Russell and his family were seen as anti-racist with the Ambrose case not mentioned or, when it was, mentioned only as among efforts to save his properties.

About 90 percent of blacks who were a large component of the overwhelmingly black, poor, uneducated, and politically inexperienced Republican Party in southeastern North Carolina viewed Daniel Jr. favorably because of the pro–civil rights decision. He became influential in Republican politics as a member of a small circle of men called the "Wilmington Ring" by the Democratic leadership. Given the demographics, the well-to-do and educated businessmen who were Wilmington Ring members controlled the party in the counties constituting the Cape Fear region.

Politics in North Carolina became an increasingly toxic backdrop to the Ambroses' and their relatives' lives over the years into the twentieth century. Russell's machinations helped create conditions for the Wilmington massacre of 1898. The Democratic Party's reliance on racism constituted the chief threat to Republican efforts to regain elective offices and to the improvement of black lives. In 1876, Russell was reelected to the North Carolina House of Commons from Brunswick, his home county, which had a white majority of about 60 percent. But to win statewide, he and other Republicans needed to find a way to carry counties with large white majorities.

When the Panic of 1873 led desperate farmers to abandon the Democrats for the Greenback Party's emphasis on debt problems, racial appeals and suppressing the black vote became temporarily muted. But any relief blacks felt was temporary. In 1878, with the endorsement of both the Republican and Greenback Parties, Russell was elected to Congress. But faced with white supremacy, the national Greenback Party collapsed when the economic slide receded in the 1880s and race again became a primary issue. In 1880, Russell left politics and focused on trying to make free labor return his agricultural properties to prosperity. He mostly failed, continuing to grow cotton when the soil was not well suited for anything but rice. However, when he turned to growing rice, his losses accumulated because black workers had to be paid higher wages to make them willing to work in the paddies.

When Russell Jr. was out of politics, he proudly projected his father's contempt for any rights of the black children he had ensnared into false apprenticeships. In an 1888 article, he conceded it was true that Democrats race-baited and abused blacks. Yet, "the negroes of the South are largely savages. . . . They are no more fit to govern than are their brethren in African swamps."[15] Thereafter, when the populist movement opened the way for his political revival, his statements made fodder for his opponents to upend any black support.

With the economic depression called the Panic of 1893, farmers began a larger agrarian protest. They wanted free coinage of silver to raise crop prices. This added to the economic depression that started under Grover Cleveland (1837–1908), leading desperate farmers to leave the Democrats, which was seen as a white man's party. A coalition of Republicans and Populists, the Fusionists, in 1896 nominated Russell Jr., who won the governorship in a three-party race. Under short-lived Populist-Republican Fusion rule, about one thousand black officials, including Congressman George H. White (1852–1918), held office.

Though blacks remained a minority of elected and appointed officials, for the 1898 election, the Democratic Party campaign overtly amounted to a struggle to regain white supremacy and Democratic rule. Democratic victory would end "Negro rule" and "Negro domination." Red Shirts, reminiscent of the Ku Klux

Klan, paraded and intimidated blacks who were less likely to show up at the polls. Russell and the Populists and Republicans lost by a landslide.

Democrats kept their promises. Legislatively, they disfranchised blacks to keep them out of power but kept some of the popular education funding and business regulation that the Fusionists had enacted. But their most important strategy was to use threats and violence to force blacks to stay away from any attempt to exercise democratic representation or political influence. They concentrated on Wilmington, in which 56 percent of the city's population was black. The city had a successful black middle class of professionals and business owners, and blacks held jobs in industry on ship crews in addition to being laborers and domestic workers. There were also black aldermen, policemen, and magistrates. Much like the black community created in Tulsa, Oklahoma, which was destroyed by whites in a massacre in 1921, blacks in Wilmington had created, despite the state's segregation and discrimination and racial conflict, a cohesive community.

On November 4, 1898, the *Raleigh News & Observer* noted that the first Red Shirt parade on horseback ever witnessed in the city electrified the whites with enthusiasm and blacks with fear. The *New York Times* reported that the subsequent violence in Wilmington started when Alex Manly, editor of the local black newspaper, the *Daily Record*, published a retort to an article written by a local white woman in defense of lynching blacks to protect white womanhood. Insisting that he had disparaged white women, a white citizens committee of lawyers, businesspeople, and other "respectable citizens" demanded that Manly leave town. Fifteen blacks were called in and also given this ultimatum. A black community meeting agreed to mail a letter saying they would comply because they could not risk violence. The deadline expired before they received a response, the citizens committee announced, and four hundred armed whites went to destroy the newspaper office. Someone set fire to the building, and a rumor spread that the whites were going next to attack and burn the black neighborhood. Blacks who had arms prepared to defend themselves. When the whites ordered them to stop gathering in groups and to disperse, the panicked blacks fired at the whites. For two days, anarchy, murder, and terrorism prevailed. Many blacks left the city. Some local officers asked for federal help but were told the governor hadn't made a request. Manly escaped from the city because he was misidentified as white.[16]

A Wilmington black woman wrote anonymously to President McKinley on November 13, 1898, describing the fear and hopelessness blacks experienced with no help from the Republican president or any other source:

The Negro in this town had no arms, (except pistols perhaps in some instances) with which to defend themselves from the attack of lawless whites. On the 10th Thursday morning between eight and nine o clock, when our Negro men had gone to their places of work, the white men led by Col. A. M. Waddell, Jno. D. Bellamy, & S. H. Fishblate marched from the Light Infantry armory on Market st. to Seventh down seventh to Love & Charity Hall (which was owned by a society of Negroes and where the Negro daily press was.) and set it afire & burnt it up And firing Guns Winchesters. They also had a Hotchkiss gun & two Colt rapid fire guns. We the negro expected nothing of the kind as they (the whites) had frightened them from the polls by saying they would be there with their shot guns. So the few that did vote did so quietly. And we thought after giving up to them and they carried the state it was settled.[17]

She told him after burning the newspaper office, they

began searching every one and if you did not submit, [you] would be shot down on the spot. They searched all the Negro Churches. And to day (Sunday) we dare not go to our places of worship. They found no guns or ammunition in any of the places, for there was none. And to satisfy their Blood thirsty appetites would kill unoffending Negro men to or on their way from dinner. Some of our most worthy [illegible] Negro Men have been made to leave the City. Also some Whites, G. Z. French, Deputy Sheriff, Chief of police, Jno. R. Melton, Dr. S. P. Wright, Mayor, and R. H. Bunting, united states commissioner. We don't know where Mr. Chadbourn the Post Master is, and two or three others white. I call on you the head of the American Nation to help these humble subjects. We are loyal we go when duty calls us. And are we to die like rats in a trap? With no place to seek redress or to go with our Greiveances?

What she described was accurate; white supremacists made leading black and white political allies leave Wilmington after forcibly evicting them from office and replacing them with coup leaders. Bands of armed men, led by prominent Democrats, seized control of Wilmington. The city officials were forced to resign, the Wilmington Ring was broken up, and such a reign of terror was directed against the blacks that many who survived left, and by 1900, the county, New Hanover, had a white majority.

Russell dispatched state troops to Wilmington. But, commanded by officers who were Democrats, they helped the local white police and militia run out the blacks and take over the city. Militiamen escorted blacks to the train station at gunpoint. In the weeks after the coup, more than 2,100 blacks left Wilmington and at least 60 black men were murdered. When Russell and the

Fusionists were elected two years before, 126,000 black men had registered to vote in North Carolina. Four years after the 1898 riot, only 6,100 black men had registered.[18]

President McKinley, briefed about Wilmington, met with Booker T. Washington, and did nothing. His lack of concern was attributed to a fear that white Southerners would have just engaged in more violence against blacks if they hadn't left. But after all, Russell Jr., still governor, did not ask for federal troops or declare a state of emergency, despite the fact that he was a Republican who had been voted into office with the support of black North Carolinians.

Neither McKinley nor the US Congress even publicly acknowledged the violence in Wilmington. Black Americans in North Carolina, including the Ambrose family and descendants, and across the nation were fearful and frightened. Blacks at a mass meeting at Cooper Union in New York City denounced the bloodshed and federal inaction.[19] The National Afro-American Council of leading black men proposed a lynching law but also that blacks should consider migration as a solution to the race question even as some members tried to defend the McKinley administration. Republicans relied on black voters, but they needed white support for their foreign and domestic policy proposals.

To black people in North Carolina, it appeared that if blacks succeeded and stayed out of trouble, having a thriving community would not lessen their vulnerability. Indeed, it might make them more threatening to whites. Along with black people who had been part of the populist Republican coalition, Russell Jr. was destroyed. But it didn't matter. Persuaded by friends, including the tobacco business leader Benjamin Duke, Russell stayed in office until his term ended, in 1901. He had in the meantime been ruined financially along with many former wealthy planters. Large-scale rice production on the Gulf Coast, using mechanized harvesting, which did not work on the Lower Cape Fear soil, took over the field.

While these changes took place in the regional economy, politics, and race relations, the Ambrose and Saunders families and their descendants struggled to recover from the exploitation and deprivation they experienced. They continued to lack resources to accumulate property and obtained an inferior segregated education, if any at all was available.

Having emerged from slavery with nothing, none of them became particularly well-off, though two of the second-generation males were described as carpenters, which may have been part of their building and maintenance work as slaves. The males served in the military or at least registered for the draft. There's no record of any of them being punished for illegal activity. They mostly stayed in North Carolina, though a few took working-class jobs such as porter in New York City and one in coastal Virginia. None were entrepreneurs or reported college-going, and there's no record of anyone finishing high school or attending college. They died of stroke, diabetes, and other diseases that still plague black people today. They were poor but free and, for the most part, maintained family ties and supported themselves and each other. Perhaps most importantly, despite obstacles, they maintained the family ties their ancestors braved odds to keep.

CHAPTER 5

FIGHTING FOR THE SONS OF SAMUEL AND OLIVER ADAMS

In 1867, Samuel Adams refused to quit until he regained custody of his three sons—Tucker, Francis, and Zachariah—from William H. Adams, his former enslaver. William Adams had stolen the children from another planter in a neighboring county to whom they had been apprenticed by their father. This was a case of white plantation owners suing for "ownership" of black youth using parents as proxies.

Samuel Adams's story is not unusual. What is atypical is its capture in the records of the Supreme Court of Georgia, courtesy of the labor demands of competing white planters. Adams and his wife had married on the Adams plantation in early 1850 (though as enslaved persons, their marriage was not recognized by law). After the Civil War, they continued to live as husband and wife and had six children still living with them: Tucker, born in 1854; Francis, born in 1855; and Zachariah (Zach), born in 1856. They had three more children "too young for field work." They remained on William Adams's plantation in Baker County until the boys' mother died.[1]

Samuel remarried in less than a year. His new wife lived in Dougherty County, on the plantation of Robert A. Dykes, where

Samuel and his children relocated. His three older sons were apprenticed as farmworkers to Dykes, who paid Samuel $150 for a year of their labor. That money helped to support his new wife and three younger children.

William Adams was enraged when Samuel and his children left. He kidnapped Tucker, Francis, and Zachariah from the Dykes plantation and put them back to work on his plantation, filing an indenture contract in the county courthouse. He claimed that Samuel was unreliable and a degenerate who'd had relations with multiple women and couldn't prove the children were his. The Baker County court judged the children illegitimate, likely to become public charges, and assigned their care to William Adams. Dykes, Samuel Adams's new employer, challenged the decision and hired a lawyer to appeal the case to the state supreme court. His motivation was not altruistic. Dykes had hired Samuel Adams because he had three sons who would also work on his property.[2]

Adams's actions on behalf of his children were shaped by a system that refused to recognize the sanctity of a black person's marriage. An earlier wife may have been sold away; another had died. He recognized his children and he tried to hold them tight. Samuel struggled to keep his family together in the face of white planters who only valued his children for the labor they could perform. Yet, in the ensuing decades, better-off black people would denigrate the efforts of other poor black families in the "heart of the Black Belt."[3] W. E. B. Du Bois, during his tenure in Atlanta, conducted research in Dougherty County on "the remnants of the vast plantations." He described what he saw: "How curious a land is this, how full of untold story, of tragedy and laughter, and the rich legacy of human life; shadowed with a tragic past, and big with future promise!" The county, he concluded, was "the center of the Negro problem, [a place where] America's dark heritage from slavery and the slave-trade" created "careless ignorance and laziness here, fierce hate and vindictiveness there."

Of the 1,500 African American families in the county in 1898, many lived in one- or two-room homes with eight to ten people. Even Du Bois seemed to dismiss the pervasiveness of white supremacy and institutionalized racism, emphasizing how these souls suffered from the plague of "easy marriage and easy separation." Almost a century later, the Dougherty seat of Albany would become a major venue in the freedom struggle as blacks engaged in nonviolent protest trying to end segregation and gain the right to vote. But the seeds of the movement had been planted long before.

Georgia, like other ex-Confederate states, passed an apprentice law in 1866 to facilitate planters' efforts to keep slave children as free labor on their plantations. But Samuel, with the assistance of Dykes, who wanted the children to work for him, cited the same law to challenge William Adams's supposed apprenticeship of his three sons. However, Baker County probate judge Benjamin F. Hudspeth accepted William Adams's claim that apprenticing the children to him fit within the law's required statement that the children "were orphans, and left without any provision for their support, and were likely to become a charge to said county," thus affirming [William Adams's] "duty and obligation to clothe and educate them, and his power as guardian over them according to law."[4] Hudspeth determined that the children were illegitimate and likely to become a public charge.

County court judge David A. Vason (1818–1891) held a trial to review Samuel Adams's complaint that his sons were not orphans or unsupported and had been given to William Adams erroneously and found no fault with the indenture to William Adams. This was not surprising. Judge Vason was very much involved in the effort of ex-Confederates to restore as much of slavery and white supremacy as possible. The Vasons were among the most influential Dougherty County families. Vason House, built in 1855, remains "the most important architectural landmark in Albany, and one of the most significant surviving Greek Revival homes in Southwest Georgia."[5] Judge Vason, a long time Dougherty County slaveholder, was the grandfather of one of Georgia's most prominent architects, Edward Vason Jones (1909–1980), who grew up in the house. A photograph dated 1910 of the infant Edward, with his African American nurse, is in the Georgia Archives. Her name, Liela Perkins, is even recorded, though often the identification of blacks in photos and portraiture, even from the twentieth century, remain unknown or unmentioned. David Vason served in the Confederate military and was pardoned after the war by President Andrew Johnson in August 1865.

Judge Vason's decision appeared reasonable because the witnesses for slave owner William Adams included two of his formerly enslaved workers. They, like many others who did not leave immediately after abolition because they didn't know they were free or had no place to go, still lived on William Adams's farm. One of the witnesses was Samuel's brother Silas. Both of the former slaves agreed that Samuel was "a great run-about after the women," was unreliable, and probably could not prove the children were his.[6]

Samuel Adams, backed by Robert Dykes, pushed the case on appeal to the state supreme court, which reversed the decision, declaring the indenture illegal. Chief Justice Hiram Warner (1802–1881) was not a Northern carpetbagger who just stayed on during Reconstruction seeking to seem moderate by ex-Confederates. He was a local. Though a native of Massachusetts, he had been in Georgia since 1822. He married a woman whose family owned a plantation and numerous slaves. Perhaps his experiences made him immune to a romantic view of slavery. He had practiced law, been a local judge, and served on the state supreme court once before, and then in the legislature and the US Congress. A delegate to the Georgia Secession Convention, he opposed secession but then, like others who "followed their state," signed the ordinance when it passed.

Chief Justice Warner's opinion deftly managed to satisfy the Republicans to whom he owed his appointment and his own inclinations. He relied on the trial court record, showing that Samuel and the mother of the children not only had married after abolition, when it became legally possible for slaves, but both acknowledged the children as theirs. Warner concluded from the trial record that Samuel "knew the children are his; he always claimed them, and said mother always called them his."[7] He regarded Samuel's position as that of a father claiming the legitimacy of his parental responsibility over his children and a power to protect his authority from the former master. The mother's death only meant that the father had control of the children and could not have his rights voided by the arguments that he was unreliable having had relationships with other women. In fact, often slaves had companions who died or were sold away. When the mother of the children at issue died, Samuel arranged for their care.[8]

But Warner pointed out a more obvious basis for his decision for Samuel Adams: the children were not residents of Baker County when the decision appealed was made. They were residents of Dougherty County, to which their father, Samuel, took them a short time before Christmas in 1866, after their mother died. The fact that he hired them to Dykes for 1867 meant "there is no pretext that they would become chargeable to the County of Baker for their support and maintenance. This act of the County-Judge, binding these children as Apprentices to defendant, was simply void, a mere nullity, and may be attacked whenever and in whatever way it is sought to be used as a valid act."[9]

Once freed to earn wages for his labor, Samuel's son Tucker ended up, in 1870, working as a field hand for J. D. Lee and lived on the Lee property in Effingham, Georgia, near the North Carolina border. Tucker married Patsy Dancy in 1877 in Sumter County, Alabama, when he was twenty-two years old. Zach Adams and his wife, Rebecca, lived in in Cross Plains, northwestern Carroll County, Georgia, toward Atlanta from Albany. They had seven children, three of whom were old enough to work on the farm Zach bought but had been mortgaged in 1910. Zach still farmed in 1930 but had remarried. His daughter, Anice Adison, was a forty-one-year-old domestic. She died on September 9, 1929, in Carroll County, having convulsions while in childbirth. The family "Dr. called but never came"; she died at 11 a.m.[10]

Formerly enslaved Oliver Adams, like Samuel Adams, contended with what Du Bois described as "fierce hate and vindictiveness" in Dougherty County as he fought to free his fourteen-year-old-son, Jesse Morris, from the slavery of a supposed apprenticeship.[11] His fight, like that of Violet Maples's and of Samuel Adams's, ended on appeal in the state supreme court.[12]

Oliver Adams retrieved Jesse from plantation owner William McKay, who tried to keep him against the will of Jesse and his father and mother, another McKay slave. William McKay, born in 1826, migrated to the States from England in 1865 where he was employed as a dyer in 1861. He and his wife, Maria, born in 1830, had five children as of 1870; the oldest was Esther and the youngest, ten-month-old Jonathan. He became a "farmer" and not a slave plantation owner by 1870, but in later years he became a minister.[13]

McKay called Jesse the "illegitimate child" of Oliver Adams's wife, Maxey, born long before their legal post-abolition marriage. McKay insisted, without proof, that he had Maxey's consent to take Jesse, age fourteen, as an apprentice and that he had kept him as a house servant, "greatly to the improvement of the minor, that he feels attached to said minor, and had, at the request and entreaty of the minor, and his election, had him bound to the petitioner as his apprentice."[14] Former slaveholders almost routinely insisted that a child they sought as an apprentice wanted to stay with them and even begged to do so.

Oliver Adams, according to McKay, only wanted to hire out Jesse to make a profit. Oliver Adams testified that, as in other cases in which a former master influenced a child to stay with them, Jesse "was over persuaded to importune" McKay to have Jesse indentured to him "but is now anxious to live with his mother." Further, Oliver insisted that Jesse had "never been a charge upon anyone except his mother and is now able to support himself." Oliver denied that his interest in Jesse was to "hire him out for gain."

The case came to trial when Georgia politics and Reconstruction offered to Oliver Adams the same trial judge Samuel Adams had: white supremacist and prominent ex-Confederate David Vason. The outcome was the same. Vason decided that McKay had a valid apprenticeship even though Oliver Adams had given no consent.

But Oliver Adams's appeal, like Samuel Adams's, came when political reality had changed. The Republican takeover of the state legislature meant that now Oliver Adams might hope for a favorable outcome. Sure enough, the state supreme court, in an opinion by Judge Dawson A. Walker (1819–1881), reversed Vason's opinion. Walker, a graduate of East Tennessee University in Knoxville (1843), practiced law in Dalton, Georgia. He had owned one slave in 1860, a ten-year-old black female in his household. Walker had a rocky political career. He was a delegate to the National Union Convention in Philadelphia in August 1866, after agreeing with Joseph E. Brown, the outgoing Confederate governor, that the state should accept Congressional Reconstruction. Then, in May 1871, when he was the Republican State Convention candidate for governor and a delegate to the Republican National Convention, former governor Brown and ex-Confederate allies abandoned him. He lost in the wake of Republican losses in the 1870 election, when Democrats took over the state's politics and government.[15]

Producing an opinion that would cancel McKay's apprenticeship of Jesse Morris was legally uncomplicated. Walker pointed out that the 1866 law let the judge, called an Ordinary, indenture minors whose parents lived outside the county, or all minors whose parents could not support them. But not only did Jesse's mother reside in the county, "there was no evidence that she was unable to support him."[16] Also, illegitimacy was totally irrelevant because the Ordinary also had no authority to apprentice "an illegitimate without the consent of the mother, unless she be unable to support her child, or some other legal reason be shown why she should be deprived of the custody of it."

Oliver Adams and Samuel Adams won their cases, but political turmoil and violence continued in Dougherty County, where the seat of Albany, a century later, was again a site of the continuation of the seemingly never-ending black freedom struggle. Ex-Confederates insisted on taking over again. As campaigns for the November 1868 state legislature election began, candidates, some of whom were carpetbaggers, urged blacks to convene rallies for their choice of candidates. Blacks who marched to the courthouse in Camilla, twenty-five miles south of Albany, for a rally were warned away by a white man who rode by, but they pressed on. When they arrived later that day, armed whites waited, and on September 19, 1868, at least a dozen blacks were killed outright and others injured as they ran into the woods.

Judge David Vason, as if his venomous approval of returning Jesse Morris and the sons of Samuel Adams back to slavery was not enough, stoked the fires of hatred outside the court. He and three other prominent whites from Albany went to Camilla and procured a statement from the local sheriff, Mumford Poore, and eight other "men of good character" that the "disturbance" in which blacks were killed was caused by armed blacks "led on by wicked white men."[17] The statement was printed in the *Albany News* and widely distributed, whereupon the Georgia legislature announced agreement with it less than a week after the massacre. Thereafter, unsurprisingly, fear of violence continued in the state; few blacks showed up for elections in the surrounding counties that had helped the Redeemers, the Southern wing of the Democratic Party, succeed in their takeover.

Oliver Adams managed to become an owner instead of a sharecropper. By 1880 he had 140 tilled and 41 untilled woodland acres and fields, and his son Adam had 75 tilled acres. He and his wife and children did not hire laborers but worked the land themselves, along with other family members.[18]

Unlike the scant records of Samuel Adams's sons and their descendants, more details are available about the Oliver Adamses. Jesse moved from place to place in Georgia, working as a farm laborer, and eventually landed in Macon. Through migration and access to education, among the laborers, cab drivers, and domestic servants, Jesse's daughters, Susie and Josephine, held jobs as public school teachers and secretaries. Josephine's daughter, also named Josephine, was a secretary in the racially segregated school system of Washington, DC, in 1950 and had married Alen Walton, who was a Veterans Administration clerk.

Oliver Adams's fight to keep his son Jesse from remaining enslaved by their former owner under the guise of an apprenticeship was a major landmark in the Adams family's history after slavery. The conflict occurred because, like other former slave owners trying to keep unpaid workers, McKay wanted Jesse to continue working for free as a house and body servant. However, Oliver couldn't see how that arrangement was any different from slavery, which he understood was over. Adams knew he had not consented to McKay's taking his child's person and labor from him, and he was determined to free him.

CHAPTER 6

THE CASE OF SARAH LACY

I f you thought that even if slavery was not abolished by the Emancipation Proclamation or even the ratification of the Thirteenth Amendment, then for sure it was ended in Texas by "Juneteenth" on June 19, 1865, consider the case of Sarah Lacy. The story began on the Timmins' plantation when Sarah Lacy, probably under age twenty, got married, "after the usual historical fashion of negro marriages, to one Harry Pope, also a negro, both being then slaves."[1] They had three children—two boys, Elkin and Chuff, and a girl, Leney—before the relationship foundered.

When she and her later husband, Moses, left the Timmins' place in 1866 with Elkin and Chuff, they hired them to George W. Pearson for that year. Although Pearson said he got the oral consent of the boy's father, Harry Pope, to the hiring, the next day, Robert Timmins, Mary Timmins's son, "went to Pearson's house with a double-barreled gun, and took the children forcibly back to Timmins' house claiming they had a labor contract." Then, "when the children went back to their mother they were again taken away by said Robert Timmins."[2]

Mary Timmins (Timmons) was the head of a slaveholding family that migrated from Tennessee to Texas in the 1840s, landing in Cherokee County, named for the Indigenous people expelled from the area. When her husband, James, died in 1859, his will directed that she, insofar as possible, "keep the negroes together."[3] There were sixteen blacks still in bondage in the last pre-Civil War slave census, in 1860. Mary Timmins chose to ignore abolition, thereafter, by acting as if she still owned Sarah Lacy's children. Of the sixteen slaves on Mary F. Timmins's plantation in Cherokee County, eight were males and eight were females. The oldest male was thirty-five and the oldest female, thirty-four. Among them were likely the former slaves involved in the apprenticeship case. Most of the slaves were under twenty, and the youngest were three males, ages two, three, and four.

Sarah Lacy managed to free her children from kidnapping back into slavery by Mary Timmins, and thereafter Moses and Sarah and their descendants maintained a working-class existence, and family ties much like others, whether they won or lost. But the backlash against abolition and justice for freed people, including terrorist violence, kept their lives uneasy.

After General Gordon Granger's June 19, 1865, "Juneteenth" announcement of emancipation, former Confederates still captured blacks and returned them to their former enslavers. Also, some owners killed those who attempted to act as if they were free. As no longer 3/5ths persons, these people chose to exercise a right to life, liberty, and the pursuit of happiness. One observer described the Sabine River, which borders Texas and Louisiana, where the Union had been in control since 1862, as running red with the blood of the murdered formerly enslaved. Susan Merritt of Rusk Country, Texas, said: "Lots of Negroes were killed after freedom . . . bushwhacked, shot down while they were trying to get away. You could see lots of Negroes hanging from trees in Sabine bottom right after freedom. They would catch them swimming across the Sabine River and shoot them."[4] After Granger's order, the Union Army had to march across Texas to enforce the order and free re-enslaved black people. Rather than allow them their freedom, "they killed as many as 2,500. They were just murdered outright across the state."

In September 1865, the Freedmen's Bureau commissioner, General Oliver O. Howard, had characterized Texas's political climate as "seem[ing] at the time . . . to be the post of great-est peril."[5] Howard recalled that little had changed a year later when the state's bureau commander, General Joseph B. Kiddoo, "found little respect for any law in the northeast counties." He explained that the Texas legislature had not ratified the federal 1866 "Civil-Rights-Law"; consequently, freedmen could not yet testify in courts of law. In fact, as a federal law, it did not need ratification, but having to pass it over President Johnson's veto, refusal to enforce it, and questions about its validity led the Republicans to enact the Fourteenth Amendment, which was ratified to achieve the same objectives as the Act. Kiddoo's "chief troubles" were the white supremacists who thwarted the Texas bureau chief's "efforts to protect [the freedmen] from violence." The plan: to "entreat . . . more troops for those remoter districts." After slavery was abolished, Harry Pope and Sarah Lacy, assum-ing they were free to do so, both remarried.

Ironically, the fact that she and Harry could not legally marry when they were slaves helped Sarah keep custody of her children when Mary Timmins claimed they were her apprentices. Sarah married Moses Lacy, by whom she had three more children, although the 1866 Texas Black Code, like not permitting black testimony, did not permit black marriages, though marriages are contracts and were permitted under the Civil Rights Act of 1866, which they ignored. Essentially, "Texas acted as if it was a law unto itself."[6]

The discriminatory Black Code allowed former slave owners needing labor to more easily use the apprenticeship law, passed on October 27, 1866. Like apprenticeship laws in other states, it required parental consent, a minor being "indigent or vagrant," or parents who had "not the means, or who refuse to support" their children. If there were no legal parents, these provisions were irrelevant. The discriminatory Black Code, which violated the Civil Rights Act of 1866 and the Fourteenth Amendment, ratified in 1868, and which sanctioned abuse, remained in place until Republicans gained control of the state legislature in 1870.

Mary Timmins said she had Harry Pope's written consent to apprentice his three children to her. She kept them on her plantation as unpaid child laborers. According to the court papers, filed at the end of December 1866, they were "to learn the vocation of farming," even though they were quite accustomed to field labor.[7] But Timmins could not have had their father's signature, because he could neither read nor write. The document filed with the court read: "Witness my hand, this the 27th day of December 1866. HARRY his X mark POPE."

The enslaver's promise to the illiterate Harry Pope included a condition that she would give each apprentice one hundred acres of land when they reached twenty-one years of age, provided they finished their apprenticeship. A small portion of Harry's biography was included in the document. Harry had been forcibly long separated from his children when he was sold away, but he nonetheless visited them. When emancipation came, he agreed to let Mrs. Timmins keep the children in 1866 and then subsequently in 1867 and 1868, if she wished. Timmins would pay Harry for the children's services. The document on which Harry made his mark claimed, "Mary B. Timmins was and is a very worthy and competent person to have the control, education, and raising of said children."

The children's mother, Sarah, and her second husband, Moses Lacy, wanted nothing to do with the Timmins plantation after

being freed from slavery. They wanted to make their own decisions. The apprenticeship to Timmins was not only years long
until age twenty-one for males and age eighteen or until married
for females; it also gave the holder of the indenture full power
to punish or correct the child without intervention from a court
or any government agency.

The Lacys complained to the Freedmen's Bureau, which did
not begin operations in Texas until July 1865, three months after
its establishment. The bureau sought to cancel the apprenticeships and retrieve the children still at the Timmins' place and
others whom planters had kept. Bureau officials saw the Texas
Apprenticeship Code as aiding the theft of black children from
their parents as they analyzed complaints and organized support
to cancel apprenticeship agreements and return children to their
parents. Taking a sterner position than in other states, the Texas
bureau insisted that only one black parent had to provide evidence of parentage and the ability to care for a child who would
not become a charge on the state to retain custody.

Harry Pope said that Sarah had agreed to work for Mary B.
Timmins and had hired herself and the children to her for 1866.
However, she and Moses Lacy decided to leave in December
1865, when the Thirteenth Amendment was ratified, abolishing
slavery, despite his agreement to let Mrs. Timmins keep the
children.

As the case proceeded, the Lacys proved that they had been
hiring out successfully, naming the employers and detailing their
profits and expenses. Hiring out to someone who the parents
trusted meant that, unlike with the state apprenticeship provisions, if abuse occurred, they could go to court or to the bureau,
and the tenure was short-term.[8]

Moses and Sarah explained to the district court that when
they left the Timmins place for Harmon Carlton's in 1866 with

their sons, Elkin and Chuff, they hired the boys to George W. Pearson for that year. Although Pearson apparently got the oral consent of Harry Pope for the hiring, the next day was when Robert Timmins, Mrs. Timmins's son, went to Pearson's house with a double-barreled gun and took the children forcibly back to the Timmins' house, claiming they had a labor contract. At the end of 1866, the children went back to live with their mother, and Timmins came and forcibly took them again in January 1867, bringing an order from the county court saying that his mother could keep Elkin Pope and Chuff Pope, considered freed minors, and keep them safely until the last Monday in January 1867, at which time Sarah would bring said minors before the county court for a decision. The trial court acknowledged that Sarah and Moses Lacy were financially able to pay their debts. Further, the Lacys, with the help of their children, could support their families and their children would not become public charges. There was no reason to uphold the apprenticeship.

On Mary Timmins's appeal to the state supreme court, an opinion by Chief Justice George Moore in April 1867 found that Sarah Lacy, the mother, was the natural guardian of her children, revoked the order of the county court, ordered the children to the care of the mother, and gave a judgment for costs. Moore had a successful law practice in Crockett, Texas, before he served briefly as a colonel in the Texas cavalry during the Civil War. He was elected an associate justice of the Texas supreme court in 1862. In 1866, he was again elected to the court but was removed in 1867 when Texas was placed under federal military authority to implement Reconstruction. He returned to practicing law, this time in Austin, and was licensed to practice in the US Supreme Court in 1870.

This is when slaves' inability to marry worked in Sarah Lacy Pope's favor. In rejecting Timmins's appeal, Chief Justice Moore noted that the apprenticeship arrangement seemed to be approved by Harry Pope in opposition to the acknowledged mother. However, he wrote, "it is a universally recognized principle of common law, that the father of a bastard has no parental power or authority over such illegitimate offspring." The maternal parent wins, and Mary Timmins loses.[9]

Perhaps Sarah Lacy and Harry Pope both had the best interests of their children in mind. She used the contract scheme established by the Freedmen's Bureau, which gave them resources and some freedom to work. If Harry indeed actually agreed to the "arrangement" with Mrs. Timmins, perhaps he wanted the children to obtain the land she promised and to live stably at her plantation until age twenty-one. He was perhaps choosing what he thought in the long term was in his children's best interests, but that forced reliance on Mrs. Timmins to keep her promise. He perhaps could not see Sarah's way as likely to give them a better future. Sarah had no reason to trust the former slave owner who had sent her son to threaten them with a double-barreled gun to coerce them.

Sometime before the 1870 US census, Sarah Lacy died. In 1870, former slaveholder Mary Timmins lived with her three sons and a daughter on her farm. There were four blacks working for the family: Bush, twelve (Chuff), and Susan, thirteen, both domestic servants; Abraham, thirty-five, and Elkin, whose age was disputed in the court case was recorded as nineteen, both of whom were farmworkers; and Henry, twenty-three, "mulatto," who also worked on the farm. Like other canvassers, the census taker that year apparently assumed the fact that they had been slaves meant their last name was Timmins. Elkin had moved elsewhere after marrying in 1873 in Cherokee. Mary Timmins became ill and died in 1881. As Bush matured, with his father living with his other family, he left the Timminses'. By 1900, Bush probably Chuff) Timmins, a farm laborer, still lived in Cherokee with his wife, Mary, and their young children, five daughters and two sons. No record exists that any of the former slaves were ever given or inherited any land or anything else from the Timmins'.

After he lost the 1867 state supreme court case to the mother of his children, Sarah Lacy, Harry Pope, in 1870, remained a farm laborer in Cherokee County, Texas. He lived with Rachel Pope, age thirty, as a presumed spouse and several of their young children. But by 1880, Harry was no longer with them, and Rachel had married James Thacker, ten years younger than Harry Pope and who worked on a farm. Her children lived with them along with four of Thacker's children.

As the Lacys and Popes tried to adjust and manage their lives after the decision, they, like other blacks, experienced the threat of and actual lynchings and anti-black violence from Redeemers who persisted in the South. After the Lacys retrieved their children, ex-Confederates took power, ending Reconstruction, which persisted into the early twentieth century. For example, on June 20, 1910, in Cherokee County, the horrific, widely publicized lynching of Leonard Johnson, who had been charged with the murder of a white woman, took place.[10]

The sheriff and his deputies offered the common excuse of the period of his being taken from them saying they were overpowered by a mob of about 150 on the way to the jail. They announced he had confessed, and then the mob led him to a stake and burned him to death. The sheriff said he did not recognize any of the participants and made no further attempts to discover who they were.[11] The next month, on July 29, 1910, the too usual aftermath of such episodes of the period occurred as several white mobs systematically shot and killed unarmed black people in the area. E. R. Bills, a Fort Worth–based writer, wrote about the subject in Texas newspaper articles before publishing the book *The 1910 Slocum Massacre: An Act of Genocide in East Texas*.[12] Bills maintains that this Slocum Massacre "compares to others such as the Rosewood Massacre in Florida and the Tulsa Race Riot of 1921, which left up to 300 people dead." Families who escaped in fear could not bury their dead. On August 1, 1910, the *Houston Post*, reported how a dozen farmers gathered to bury decomposed bodies in a mass grave, to protect the public health. As a result, the number of blacks killed remains uncertain. Observers guessed between eighteen and forty. But indisputably no white person was even injured "during the trouble." What happened there was just part of the well-documented lynching and racial violence, of the period that blacks had to endure to survive after Reconstruction was overturned.

The Popes and Lacys, like other formerly enslaved people, tried to avoid the racial violence from the Redeemers as they persevered. They were farm laborers or domestics, suffered similar illnesses with uncontrolled diabetes, high blood pressure, and kidney disease. In other families, someone somehow ended up in the state hospital for the "feeble-minded" or someone might get into trouble for "stealing" a hog to provide food in hard times.

CHAPTER 7

SAVING SIMON MITCHELL

In 1871, in Bulloch County, Georgia, John McElvin, like other planters, wanted to keep unpaid labor as long as possible after the abolition of slavery.

Like other towns and counties, instead of naming the county for the Indigenous people who were driven out of the area, the settlers named it for Archibald Bulloch (1730–1777), the president and commander in chief of Georgia in 1776 and the state's first provisional governor. Founded in 1786, Bulloch County is thirty miles west of Savannah, and in the nineteenth century was populated by planters, timbermen, and turpentine distillers from Ireland and England. As elsewhere, they followed the Muskogean or Creek people's trading trails and paths to create wagon trails and cleared land for farms and plantations.

McElvin (1814–1890) owned one slave in 1850, a Filipino, age twenty-two, who may have been among the escapees from Spanish ships traveling from New Spain to Mexico. In 1860, he had eight black slaves—four males, ages forty, fourteen, nine, and five; four females, age thirty-two, fourteen, seven, and one—and sought to retain as much as he could of his pre-abolition assets. One goal McElvin had was to arrange an apprenticeship of fourteen-year-old Simon Bissett. The case ended eventually in the state supreme court case *Mitchell and Lee v. McElvin* (1872).

During slavery, Simon's father, Simon Lee, and his mother, Sophia Bissett, were owned by different planters, however, they lived together as husband and wife "after the manner of slaves, for many years, and during this period the boy Simon was born."[1] They also had another younger child who was not yet old enough to be a good worker and for whom McElvin made no claim.[2]

Simon Lee sought legal intervention to oppose the apprenticeship during a period of political and social turmoil. Bulloch County's cotton-based economy depended on slavery, and by 1850, the enslaved people constituted a third of the county's population, and by 1860, nearly half. The Civil War did not bring a major battle to the county, though the planters generally supported the Confederacy. After the war, as ex-Confederates sought to regain control of the state, blacks who engaged or who were thought to engage in Republican politics and carpetbaggers suffered injury and death, as in the Camilla Massacre of 1868.[3]

McElvin obtained an order from the local probate court giving him custody of the boy and claiming that the child's mother, Sophia Bissett, had agreed to an indenture to him. When the boy's father, Simon Lee, objected, McElvin simply ignored him.

However, Simon Lee had black friends, some of whom had long been free, who knew how he might defeat McElvin and free his son. In Savannah, blacks, free and enslaved, had a long history of engagement in skilled and unskilled labor. They were accustomed to supporting themselves, and some free people of African descent were well-to-do. By abolition, in 1865, black skilled artisans, trained as slaves by owners to hire out at higher rates than ordinary hands, lived among black drayage, rice-mill, and construction workers and as municipal employees in the neighborhoods, as reported by the 1870 census and thereafter. Slaves had been members of black firefighting companies and peddlers of fruits, vegetables, and flowers. The small number of free people of African descent, 705 in 1860, including William M. Mitchell, also worked at these occupations.[4]

Mitchell, a successful "mulatto" street vendor agreed to have his friend Simon Lee bypass McElvin by apprenticing his son to him. This was not unusual. Before the Civil War, local probate judges would permit a free black parent to choose a friend or a person who would educate or train their child well when ordering apprenticeship when the parent could not afford child support.

Mitchell (1840–1893), born in and residing his entire life in Chatham County, had a peddler license and lived mostly in Savannah. Before the war, in 1860, Mitchell was among 705 free Negroes living in the city. Mitchell and Simon Lee took young Simon from McElvin's place, where he was still living in 1870 as a farm laborer, to live with Mitchell.[5]

McElvin reacted by filing a habeas corpus suit against Lee and Mitchell before Chatham County judge William Schley in August 1871, asking Mitchell and Simon's father to return Simon, age fourteen, to his custody. Schley descended from an accomplished family that had emigrated from Germany in 1745 to Maryland and then moved to Georgia in the nineteenth century. Schley was governor of Georgia (1835–1837) and also, along with his brother Jacob, succeeded in the railroad and cotton mill business. They erected the second and third cotton mills in Georgia.[6]

At trial, Simon Lee testified that, having become "involved in a difficulty," he ran away from McElvin's plantation, and when he returned, Sophia refused to live with him. When the Union Army came through Bulloch County, Sophia and her children moved to Bryan County. About three years before the trial, Simon Lee visited them and offered to help her take care of the children, though he had married another woman, which was not unusual given the conditions of slavery.[7]

According to the Judge Schley's summary of the trial court testimony, Simon Bissett's mother, Sophia, wanted her son to stay under the control of his father and refused McElvin's repeated requests to apprentice Simon to him. Then McElvin threatened her, saying he would "run the boy off to Florida unless she acquiesced."[8] He also told her that the boy "was badly treated" by his father, Simon Lee, and "would not live with anyone" except McElvin. Under his threats, she signed the deed of apprenticeship but repeatedly told him she had given Simon to his father and didn't want to sign the apprenticeship papers.

When McElvin introduced a deed of apprenticeship for Simon Bissett, supposedly signed by his mother on May 31, 1871, to show his right to the custody of the boy, Mitchell and Simon Lee objected. Aside from the threats, the articles had apparently not been filed in the probate office, as required. Judge Schley ignored the objections, including Sophia's claim of Duress, and gave custody to McElvin.

In 1872, after Mitchell and Simon Lee appealed, the Supreme Court of Georgia, in an opinion by Judge William Watts Montgomery, reversed Judge Schley's decision and left the child with his father, Simon Lee, and William W. Mitchell.[9] Montgomery, a Confederate supporter, focused only on the legislation involved, explaining that under still existing state child-custody law enacted during Military Reconstruction, "a colored child, born before the 9th day of March 1866, within what was regarded as a state of wedlock between its parents, while slaves, and who is acknowledged by its father, is the legitimate child of both parents."[10]

If the parents had separated before that date and the minor child remained with the mother, she controlled the child. But if she voluntarily yielded control to the father, and he took the child away, she couldn't take control again unless the father agreed. Sophia had voluntarily given custody to the legitimate father. Further, the child should have stayed with Mitchell and Lee, "especially where the mother testifies that she does not desire to withdraw the child from the custody of the father, and that she was induced to sign the articles by the representations made to her."[11]

After the case was decided, Simon called himself Simon Mitchell after the free black man who helped him to avoid McElvin's supposed indenture. Chatham County and the Savannah labor market changes created opportunity but also constraints for entering workers like Simon Mitchell. After slavery, blacks in Savannah continued to work in the same types of jobs as before the war and new ones. While black men were working at fifty-eight different occupations in 1870, they labored at ninety-two different occupations in 1880.[12] At that time, while blacks were only 50 percent of the population, more than 50 percent of all draymen, porters, bricklayers, coopers, and cotton samplers in Savannah, from 1870 to 1880, were black. The apprenticeship of young blacks to skilled black artisans led to an increase in the percentage of blacks in the total number of shoemakers, butchers, and barbers.

As large construction companies grew, and black carpenters', plasterers', and painters' share of the workforce declined, so did the percentage in the manufacturing, mechanical, and building trades decline. However, in the 1870s, blacks working as common laborers, firemen, and engineers, on the railroads, boats, and in the factories, increased.

Many artisans, earning from $1.81 to $3.50 per day, refused to allow their wives to work. However, most black women in 1870, and 60 percent in 1880, were wage workers, as laundresses, domestic servants, and cooks.[13] Increasingly, racism left a growing percentage of black men working as laborers and domestic servants by 1880 than had been the case in 1870. Concentration in such labor in Savannah had important consequences for black men. For example, the black unemployment rate was much higher than that of whites. In 1880, blacks constituted 75 percent of the male unemployed. Of the 767 black men who were unemployed, 57 percent were common laborers, 13 percent were servants, and 4 percent were porters.

Simon Lee seemed to have trouble finding opportunities and adjusting to his new life. In 1880, at age twenty-eight, he was a laborer, and his wife, Ann, age eighteen, kept house. Their daughter, Saina, was four months old. They lived with William Mitchell and his family in Savannah on West Broad Street. William and Lydia Mitchell had six children, three girls and three boys. One daughter, Mary, was born about 1878 and died in 1880 from malaria. Only Lila, born in 1883, could read and write. The Mitchells and others in their black neighborhood were typical of the black community elsewhere in Savannah, including the prevalent social and economic conditions. Many of the women reportedly kept house, though there were a few washerwomen or servants. Several men were laborers like Simon, but others were hucksters or had a trade of some kind, or occasionally worked as a carpenter or plasterer. William and his son Arthur were reported as "mulattoes," but the others were black.

In tracing the fate of the Mitchells after William Mitchell's death in 1893, Lydia remained widowed and a washerwoman or laundress. Her children lived with her and worked variously as a huckster, peddler, or servant.

By 1900, the Mitchell family had fallen to an entirely different and lower economic-class neighborhood, renting in Wylly Ward, Duffy Street Lane West, House no. 240, no. 107. Almost all the residents were black and worked as servants, laborers on railroad or in mills, and washerwomen, except for one iceman, a seamstress, a dressmaker, and a painter. A few people reported some school attendance, but most reported they could read and write.[14]

On March 13, 1890, Arthur was convicted of disorderly conduct for assaulting Thomas O'Neill in a store one morning at 1 West Broad and New Houston Streets at 10 a.m. Punishment was five dollars and ten days in jail. He was convicted for gambling on November 26, 1892, and in June 1893, he was convicted and jailed for an unclear offense, found guilty, and discharged because of time already served. His employment was described as a huckster.[15]

By 1910, Arthur, described as "mulatto," was working as a laborer on the wharf, and Ada, his wife, born at 1 West Broad in 1883, was a laundress. They had been married nine years and had an infant son, Charlie, and a stepdaughter, Marguerite Shelton, who lived with them. When he was registered to vote in 1896, in Savannah, Arthur lived at 225 Walberg Street, a cross street of West Broad. In 1910, they rented a house at 1003 Thirty-Fourth Street, and he reportedly could read but not write.

In 1910, William Mitchell's widow, Lydia, then fifty-five, headed a household at Walburg Street Lane, in Ward 1. Her daughter Lila, twenty-six, a cook for a private family, and her son-in law, John Jones, a railway flagman, and her son, William, age twenty-four, a loader for a steamship line, lived with her. A large number of "mulattoes" lived around them, but they and only a few others were listed as black. Lydia died on May 20, 1926, apparently from a cerebral hemorrhage.[16]

Unlike most of the other youth whose apprenticeships were overturned by the courts, over the years, Simon, like Arthur, had several encounters with local Savannah law enforcement for minor offenses such as fighting in the street. Local court dockets showed disorderly conduct and fighting in the street offenses starting in 1871 through 1890. Each time, fines and some days in jail were ordered. But for a December 1875 stabbing offense, not causing death, he received a hard-labor sentence and served on the chain gang for two months.[17]

Also, Simon Mitchell, who seemed to spend a great deal of time wandering around, claimed that he had been victimized in the streets. On April 1, 1873, the *Savannah Morning News* reported that "Susan Mitchell, Mary Williams and Phillis Williams, a trio of colored females notorious in Robertsville," were arraigned in magistrate's court, charged with "cursing, abusing, and using (opprobrious) words, as the darkies say, towards an inoffensive colored biped, Simon Mitchell, by name. The charcoal blossoms were compelled to give bonds to keep the peace."

Then Simon, out on the streets again at about 11 a.m. on August 7, ran into trouble. Malvina Jones, a black "Abusive Female" engaged in disorderly conduct in the street, "cursing and abusing a colored man named Simon Mitchell." Policeman Ling "chanced along in the nick of time and carried the dusky termagant off to the barracks."[18]

Thomas, who had been a slave on the McElvin plantation and was probably Simon's brother or stepbrother, had a different experience. He stayed at the McElvins' at first and was still living there at age twenty-one, in 1870. He was a farm laborer but beyond the age of indenture, and there's no evidence as to whether he was paid for his labor. McElvin's personal estate in 1870 was $1,000 and his real estate was worth $2,000, but in 1882, he owned 332 acres of land worth only $1,000.

Thomas continued, like other freed people, to use the last name McElvin (McElveen) even after he left. He kept the name when he married Maria J. Coneariah, in Bulloch County, on March 7, 1877. He was twenty-six when, in 1880, he and Maria, age twenty-two, lived in Briar Patch in Bulloch County. He farmed, and she kept house. Thomas owned no real estate and had $278 in stock, $20 in household and kitchen goods, and $25 in plantation and mechanical tools, with an aggregate value of $318, an increase from 1874 to the 1881 value of $164.[19]

The litigation that led to Simon Mitchell's freedom from the apprenticeship did not set him on his way to a promising future, but it still gave him the opportunity to make decisions about his life. The death of William Mitchell made life for the Mitchells, including Simon, increasingly precarious.

As the Lees and Mitchells tried to make their way in freedom, they endured the seemingly incessant violence, lynchings, and other racial conflicts in Georgia, especially in the years after Republican Reconstruction was upended by ex-Confederates. Bulloch County's most infamous racial conflict, the lynching of Paul Reed and Will Cato, in 1904, was just one example. It occurred in a year when there were seventy-three lynchings in Georgia, more than any other state.[20]

In August 1904, Reed and Cato were arrested for the alleged murder of a white family; they were held in the Statesboro, Georgia, jail, supposedly "protected" by a local militia company. For some reason, the militia was armed only with bayonets and unloaded weapons. A crowd broke into the courthouse, pushed past the soldiers, took the prisoners outside town, and burned them alive. Women along the path of the mob gave the mob quart jars of kerosene. After Cato and Reed, who were chained by the neck, were covered with kerosene, women, men, and children gathered to watch while they burned to death. Some took bone fragments as souvenirs.

Obsessed, the Cato and Reed mob then embarked on the not unusual pogrom of the period: attacking innocent blacks during which at least four other additional black people in Bulloch County were killed. The terror ended only when the weary throng became exhausted. A commission appointed by the governor quickly concluded that even a regiment could not have controlled the mob. The governor had not asked for federal aid, and none was offered. A Wall Street broker wrote to President Theodore Roosevelt, asking him to send troops to arrest the lynchers. US attorney general William H. Moody replied that no federal law had been violated.[21]

W. R. Leaken, an assistant attorney general for the district involved, thought there were federal grounds for a conviction. He wrote Moody for authority to ask a grand jury, which was already in session for an indictment against the mob leaders. The attorney general responded that an indictment under federal law could be invoked only when a federally protected right was violated. In his view, the US Constitution did not protect blacks from murder. Leaken responded by sending Moody a press clipping indicating that the "best people" in the state were disgusted with lynching.[22]

Leaken also expressed his belief that the Statesboro case paralleled one in Huntsville, Alabama, in September 1904, in which a mob burned a black man, and indictments were brought in federal court. However, Attorney General Moody pointed out the differences between the two cases to Leaken: In Huntsville, when the mob burned the jail, the sheriff let the prisoner out, and the mob captured him outside the jail. The mob leaders were not indicted for murder but for burning the jail and threatening the lives of the other federal prisoners inside. Then, Judge Emory Speer, who was presiding over the jury, wrote the attorney general to ask if Leaken had authority to proceed. He was informed that Leaken had not been given that authority and had, in fact, been reprimanded for his presumptuousness.[23]

After the grand jury was discharged, the department had a change of heart and informed Leaken to proceed on his own responsibility if he so desired. Leaken, angry because now it was too late, wrote a long letter complaining about the department's vacillation. The attorney general explained that the department did not want to issue indictments every time someone was lynched because then they would likely be forced to abandon the charges.[24] There were unsubstantiated rumors that blacks were organizing to attack whites. Terrorist activity by night riders continued. Whites continued to lynch blacks for offenses such as when a father tried to defend his daughter, who was whipped for allegedly "pushing" a white person from a sidewalk. Black men took guns and hid from night riders in cotton fields while their wives and children boiled potash (lye) to use if the terrorists came to their houses. Understandably, blacks began migrating out of Bulloch County, exacerbating labor shortages for white farmers with cotton and corn crops to harvest. Some whites then tried to play down the existence of fear and violence. The Mitchells and other blacks had tried to manage a precarious existence as they sought upward mobility or opportunity in the aftermath of slavery.

CHAPTER 8

THE MYSTERIOUS FATE OF THE COMPTONS AND TILLMANS

I n 1880, Friday Compton failed to free his two sons from an illegal apprenticeship to Hiram Bruister (Brinster) (1849–1917), their former master. When a Choctaw County, Alabama, probate judge gave Ben, nineteen, and John, fourteen, to Bruister, Compton filed a habeas corpus suit hoping to retrieve them.[1]

At trial, presided over by Judge Luther Smith of the First Judicial Circuit, Bruister claimed that "when the children were apprenticed to him; they were in destitute circumstances; that they were motherless, and had been abandoned by the [Friday] appellee for several years, who had done nothing towards their maintenance and support, not even informing them where he was, or that he was alive."[2] After Friday explained his concern for the boys and that whatever difficulties he had experienced during slavery he had the "ability to support his children." Judge Smith ordered their release to him.[3]

However, Hiram Bruister successfully appealed Judge Smith's decision to the Supreme Court of Alabama, which returned Ben and John to him. Judge George Washington Stone used an earlier opinion to interpret the state 1876 apprenticeship law in reversing Friday Compton's victory. That 1872 opinion decided that the state law made apprenticeship necessary when a sheriff or other county official reported an orphan under eighteen, "without visible means of support, or whose parents have not the means, or who refuse to provide for the support of such minor." Nothing in the law required any evidence to prove or disprove what they reported, and it facilitated planters' re-enslavement of black children.[4]

That earlier opinion took the view that since, under the apprenticeship law, probate judges had to decide the facts, and when they did so, their judgment could only be attacked in another trial specifically for the purpose of determining the facts. But this meant that a petition for any appeal was denied automatically as a forbidden "collateral proceeding."[5]

The only limitation required was that the minor's father or mother must be notified if they lived in the county, since "the said minors having no parents to provide for them" was all the confirmation the apprenticeship law required. The probate judge's conclusion, based on what the reporting official said, should stand. It did not matter that Friday Compton insisted he could provide for his children and had not agreed to the apprenticeship.[6]

Judge Stone also added a more stinging rationale for his reversal of the lower court. He said the boys should never have been given to Friday Compton in the first place, and he announced that when the father seeks custody, the court can decide to ignore the father's claim if he seems "unsuitable or unable properly to care for his offspring." Despite the obvious hardships for slaves and the formerly enslaved, Judge Stone ignored Friday's testimony and accepted Bruister's description of how Friday Compton had abandoned his children "in their helpless infancy, motherless, and making no provision for their support; remained in a county not far remote from them for eight years, without letting them know where he was, or that he was living, and without even inquiring after them, so far as this record informs us. Conduct, so unnatural and unfeeling, appeals in vain for judicial assistance."[7]

Friday Compton's loss of his children was likely influenced by power and timing. Democrats took over and "redeemed" the South from Republican reconstruction in 1874 through terrorism voter suppression and racial conflict. They took control of the legislature and governor's office, wrote a new constitution in 1875, and that same year passed legislation to maintain racially segregated schools. Legislation to maintain segregation on the railroads passed in 1891, and for other public facilities, it proceeded in the years thereafter.

The Comptons were affected, like other former slaves, by the racial conflict during the determined and ultimately successful efforts of the ex-Confederates to overthrow the Republicans and install white supremacist Democratic Party control in the area. John Compton was still at the Bruisters, identified as a servant in 1874, when a group of black men resisted the overthrow by secretly organizing to support Republican candidates, including a white man, Warner Bailey, running as an independent for probate judge. They agreed to punish any of their group who leaked their plans to Democrats or anyone outside their group. When white Democrats starting harassing and threatening blacks, the black men identified Huff Cheney, who worked for a white man as the informer and whipped him as the previously agreed-upon punishment. The black men were organizing apparently under Jack Turner, whom the Democrats identified as the leader and served with an arrest warrant, issued for breaching the peace by "lynching." Cheney was still around, asking for forgiveness from the black men he had put at risk.

Rumors spread that the black men, led by Turner, were planning to kill all of the white people in the county. One of the Bruisters, J. W. [Brister], "a leading citizen "of Mount Sterling, told the local press that "Jack Turner was coming into town with a company of armed negroes, and that he intended mischief." J.W., who was Hiram Bruister's father, and four other men were delegated to confer with Jack Turner. They met Turner with about thirty of his comrades on the road. Turner said they had been summoned to court and were on their way there. Bruister asked them not to go, he said, because it would cause trouble. According to him, Jack Turner insisted that black people wanted to use the law, not just the white people who had the law before, and that those arrested should stand trial along with him and any others charged, and not alone.

The deputy sheriff arrived and said those arrested had to attend court. Turner said they would leave their weapons behind before they went into the court. Meanwhile, a white posse, which had been organized in Mount Sterling, came up behind them with the townsmen facing them. The armed blacks who had come into town because they had to appear in court were considered a threat, so the posse apparently began firing. Jack and his men escaped into the woods, as the rumors and sightings and reports of threats to kill all the whites accumulated.

Republican officeholders got federal troops sent to insure the holding of the November 1874 election. However, the Democrats swept the state and ex-Confederates retook control. The organizing of blacks and the federal troop presence helped but did not encourage black voter turnout given the violence, intimidation, and continued incarceration of Turner and the other black men who had tried to organize.

Knowing that if they languished in jail they would be in danger, Jack Turner and the other men pled guilty to the charge of lynching the informer they had beaten and were each fined five hundred dollars. The election results and the despair of having a fair result made a jury trial impractical. Jack could not pay his fine and stayed in jail until he was bailed out by sympathizers in 1875. He stayed active in Republican Party voter organizing despite the risks.[8]

Everyone knew everyone in the tiny town of Mount Sterling in Choctaw County, Alabama. With a population of only 126 persons, the Comptons, Tillmans, and other black families still lived close together after abolition. In 1882, whites responded to what was publicized in the papers, which confirmed a plot started in 1878 by blacks to "kill the entire white population" of Choctaw County.[9] Based on this latest rumor, police proceeded to arrest D. Barney, Jessie Wilson, Peter Hill, Willis Lyman, Aaron Scott, and Range West. Long-time black voter organizer Jack Turner was lynched as the supposed leader.

My research led me to the National Memorial for Peace and Justice, opened by legal advocate and law professor Bryan Stevenson in Montgomery in 2018. It's dedicated to the more than four thousand African Americans who were lynched by white Americans. On the long wall of death notices is this: "Jack Turner was lynched in Butler, Alabama, in 1882 for organizing black voters in Choctaw County."[10]

His name appears between "Jim Eastman was lynched in Brunswick, Tennessee, in 1887 for not allowing a white man to beat him in a fight" and "Elizabeth Lawrence was lynched in Birmingham, Alabama, in 1933 for reprimanding white children who threw rocks at her."

All Jack Turner and the others were doing was what he devoted himself to after abolition: working with others to organize black voters, which threatened white supremacy. The political violence in Georgia, as elsewhere, continued. When Calvin Mike was killed in 1884 in Calhoun County, Georgia, for voting, a white mob burned his house and killed his elderly mother and his two young daughters.[11]

Against the backdrop of violence and political suppression, in the 1900 US Census, Simon Tillman, a black farmer, and his family were renting a home in Mount Sterling along with the Compton family and a few others. He and his wife, Minervia, whose maiden name was Chaney, had ten children, the oldest seventeen and the youngest two and a half.[12]

In 1900, John Compton, age thirty-two, and his wife, twenty-five, still lived in Mount Sterling, Choctaw, Alabama, where the Bruisters still lived. He was likely one of the Hiram Bruister slaves whom Bruister had wanted to apprentice. John and his family rented their house and farm. The Compton children—Emily, four; Jonathan, five months; Frank, fifteen; Stephen, ten—lived by themselves as farm laborers in 1880. They were probably the remaining unaccounted-for children of Friday Compton. Mount Sterling still had only a few scattered houses.

Through the period of racial lynching and strife, in the interim between 1900 and 1910, Simon Tillman and his wife, Minervia, mysteriously were no longer in the area, and the Comptons had adopted three of their children. Simon could have been one of the arrested or driven-away black "troublemakers" J. W. Bruister helped to suppress. John Compton, born in 1865, designated by the census as a "mulatto," rented a house, farmed, and was married to Sinnie Compton for twenty-two years. She could read and write, but he could not. They had three adopted children—William, sixteen (born 1894), who worked with the Comptons on the farm; Luberta, fourteen (1895 or 1896); and Bessie Tillman, thirteen (1896 or 1897), whose parents were listed as Simon and Minervia in the 1900 US Census. John and his family lived in Choctaw Precinct 5; John died in December 1923 at age fifty-seven.[13]

Of the three adoptees, William Compton married Ada Woods, on December 21, 1916, in Lavaca, Choctaw County. He registered for the World War I draft but did not get called. In 1929, they lived in Danville, Virginia, where he was a tobacco worker. By 1930 they had moved back to Choctaw County, where they lived as farmers thereafter. Of the non-adopted children of Simon and Minervia, Julia Tillman (b. 1883) married Horace Hatcher in 1904. For a time, they lived in Mobile, Alabama, where she was a washerwoman and he was a Methodist minister.[14]

In 1880, after the case was lost, former slave owner Hiram Bruister's household consisted of his wife, Huberta (1854–1891), born in North Carolina; a four-year-old son, Hiram; and a two-year-old daughter, Mattie. Mary B. Robertson, a black female servant, age ten, lived with them, as did John Compton, who was reported as a twelve-year-old black servant. There was no record of Ben Compton thereafter in the census.

By 1940, the Bruister descendants had all finished high school and had jobs such as a clerk, beauty operator, or office supervisor. They fared well considering the loss of their slave property and land, compared to the formerly enslaved who were the basis of their economic well-being. The legal case in which Friday lost his sons to Hiram Jackson Bruister remained part of the Compton-Tillman legacy.

Those Comptons traced after the loss in the apprenticeship case were, like other blacks, freed from apprenticeships and their descendants, mainly working class, were farmers and laundresses, with an occasional man called to preach minister. The deficits of education and discrimination made it difficult for them to pursue more than poor or working-class lives. Those eligible registered for the military draft and served in the military during wartime. The mystery of Simon Tillman's fate lingered on unexplained.

CHAPTER 9

VIOLET MAPLES AND BOSS: THE FAMILY FEUD THAT WASN'T

A reader of the 1873 volume of Mississippi Supreme Court cases might be forgiven for skimming over the case of *Maples v. Maples*. At first glance it was the legal effort of a mother to maintain control of her son, Boss. At first glance, the head note of *Maples v. Maples* says it is a habeas corpus issue: one Maples complaining that another Maples has unlawfully confined someone in violation of their constitutional rights. Both parties in the case, Violet and her father, Ambrick, had recently been emancipated by the Thirteenth Amendment. Given these realities, the reader might not realize that Violet Maples and her father are merely proxies for two white planters suing each other over the "ownership" of Boss Maples, Violet's fifteen-year-old son. As with so much of African American history, reading between the lines reveals a complex story of black desires for self-determination and white exercise of racial and economic dominance. Retelling Violet's story from her perspective allows us to better understand what reparative justice means to her descendants, to others of the formerly enslaved, and to us. It also informs us about the long road the formerly enslaved trod.[1]

Though *Maples v. Maples* made it appear that Violet's father was seeking custody of Boss, the decisions of their white employers were still key to determining their futures during the post–Civil War economic upheaval and contestation between Republicans and white supremacists. Violet did not want Boss living so far away in Mississippi, staying with her father, Ambrick, and working with plantation owners there instead of returning to her in Alabama without her permission. Hers was a struggle for the recognition of family ties and self-determination, which black people have continually sought. The freedom to create and maintain a family required that the child's parents could decide that he needed to be with them; Boss's brother Henry just six years old, and Violet's two younger brothers, Silas and Prince, were twelve and ten, respectively. To be sure, as the lawyers argued, Violet and her children would have a better chance of gaining other employment and leaving the Bridgeforth plantation, where they were formerly enslaved. The labor of her sons and brothers would help support the family and the possibility of owning their own forty acres. But the court elicited no legal principles to remedy the psychological pain of separation and exploitation, a denial of their humanity imposed. Without personal freedom, emancipation from slavery remained an empty promise.

Violet's father, Ambrick, was owned by the Maples. He was born a slave in North Carolina in 1811. He was taken to Virginia, then Tennessee, and then Limestone County, near Huntsville, Alabama, where Violet was born in 1845. The white Maples were a wealthy slave-owning family who settled in Limestone County in the years before the patriarch, John W., died in 1851. His sons continued to prosper. Absalom, who died in 1848, owned nineteen slaves, according to the 1840 US Census; his brother Malcolm, born in 1818 in Limestone, according to the 1860 census, owned fifty-two slaves, including a female, age twenty-

five (who could have been Violet); a male, age fifty (probably
Ambrick); and a male age two (likely Boss). Either Malcolm or
one of his other brothers, William C., Josiah (Joe), or John W.
Jr., could have been Boss's father.

After Ambrick Maples became legally free, he settled by
1870 in northern Mississippi near Plum Point in DeSoto County,
twelve miles from Hernando, the county seat. Named for Spanish
explorer Hernando DeSoto, who allegedly died in the area in
1542, the county is on the northwest corner of Mississippi along
the Tennessee-Arkansas border, south of Memphis. The area had
seen conflict of continuous Union and Confederate raiding parties during the war. After the Union Navy defeated the Confederates on the Mississippi River, Memphis surrendered on June 6,
1862, and became a Union stronghold. Three DeSoto countians
served in the Confederate Army with the rank of general, including Nathan Beford Forrest, who led the successful destruction of
Sulphur Creek Trestle in Limestone County in 1864.

DeSoto County, between the lines of Confederate and Union
troops, suffered raids by both. In June 1863, Union troops destroyed the courthouse and main businesses in Hernando. These
troops sacked and burned buildings for five days. In 1864, Union
troops returned to burn a hotel and other buildings.

The destruction of the war led to widespread economic devastation. DeSoto County's government, like that in other places,
was bankrupt, and its agriculture base was ruined. Some local
families migrated west to Arkansas, Texas, and California. Politically, following the surrender, DeSoto County, like the rest of
Mississippi, was under Military Reconstruction, starting in 1867
with Adelbert Ames as the military governor. As happened elsewhere, the Republican governors appointed Northerners, called
carpetbaggers, and locals who cooperated with them, called
scalawags, to county political and judicial offices. Throughout

the South, white supremacist violence against black and white
Republicans raged after the Johnson presidency ended, until the
1875 election formally overthrew Reconstruction. In 1876, Adelbert Ames was replaced as governor when Democrats regained
political power.[2]

In 1873, when *Maples v. Maples* was decided, Ambrick
worked in DeSoto County on the Jeffries plantation near Horn
Lake. Violet Maples remained at the plantation of Robert Lamar
(R. L.) Bridgeforth in Limestone. The Bridgeforth-Witt House,
which he purchased in 1869, is still standing today. Although
emancipation permitted her to legally marry Thomas McWilliams, as recorded in December 1868, she is still called Violet
Maples in the court proceedings. Violet Maples is reported in
the 1870 US Census as McWilliams's wife and mother of Shoat
McWilliams (age three) and John McWilliams (age twelve). There
is no subsequent record for 1880. However, ignoring her recorded
marriage, her father told the court in *Maples v. Maples* that she
had had taken up with unnamed other men by whom she had
children. The loose woman/unfit mother charge was frequently
used by white planters who wanted to keep a black woman's
child in servitude.[3]

Acting also as if her marriage didn't exist, John W. Bridgeforth, the son of, R. L., Violet's former slave owner and now
employer, appeared as her agent in the case, sent by his father.
Violet's father, Ambrick, and mother had been R. L.'s slaves,
which made her a slave. R. L. was one of wealthy planter David Daniel Bridgeforth's three sons. David Daniel Bridgeforth
was born in Nottoway, Virginia, in 1793 and moved to Giles
County, Tennessee, where he raised his family. By 1836, he
owned more than four hundred acres worth $2,800 and ten
slaves worth $6,200. In the years before his death, in 1842, he
had sent two sons, R. L. and James William, from Giles County

to Limestone, and two other sons, Thomas and John Beverly, to DeSoto County, Mississippi, to establish their own plantations.[4]

When John Beverly died, in 1852, he made R. L. the guardian of his daughters, Mary and Lucy, and Thomas, the guardian of his sons, James William and Thomas, until they came of age. R. L. and Thomas were executors of his estate. R. L. Bridgeforth had prospered in the years since his father sent him to Alabama. In 1860, in the last US Census before the Civil War began, he owned thirteen slaves on his plantation in Limestone.

Violet first sensed that her father, Ambrick, and his employers and their friends in Mississippi were up to something when fifteen-year-old Boss didn't leave with them when she and the other children went back to Alabama. After he visited his father in Louisiana, he went back to Mississippi. Violet thought freedom meant being able to determine what would happen to her children, something her mother had never been able to do for her. She was not about to let the former planters, acting in her father's name, take that freedom away from her without a fight. She was hopeful because her former owners and employers, the Limestone Bridgeforths' interests happened to coincide partly with hers. They wanted to bring Boss back to labor on their plantation.

But Samuel Powell, a lawyer, representing the Mississippi planters in Ambrick's name, vigorously opposed her suit advanced by the Alabama planters. Powell emphasized Ambrick's testimony that Boss was better off with him because Violet was too poor and an unfit mother. Besides, Ambrick asserted, she had seven children, "all by different men." Moreover, Ambrick claimed that Boss was at least eighteen years of age and therefore could not be forced to stay with his mother.[5]

When he arrived in De Soto County, John W. Bridgforth, R. L.'s son, testified that his uncle Thomas, who still lived there and knew the Jeffries, where Ambrick worked and lived, went with him to demand Boss. John addressed the unfit-mother charge Ambrick used in court by pointing to her marriage to McWilliams. He stated that Violet had "been married to her present husband several years; has two other children, the youngest about two years of age."[6]

After Violet and the other children went home, Boss said he wandered around. Then, using the four dollars his white father gave him in Louisiana and five dollars his mother gave him from hiring out proceeds the year before, he returned to Mississippi. Boss said he worked thereafter on former Confederate captain T. P. Manning's neighboring farm, for another five dollars. He said he was content to stay in Mississippi for the time being.[7]

The Alabama Bridgeforth attorneys argued that Violet had a right to the custody of her son, who was only age fifteen and therefore had no legal right to decide where to stay in opposition to his mother. The Bridgeforths were also deeply interested in recovering Joe, another "mulatto" child who had run away to Boss in Mississippi. Though Joe had been a slave in their household until abolition, and was probably R. L's son, the Bridgeforths claimed he was an apprentice. Joe and his family's prospects and economic futures remained like those of his friend Boss. His likely father, R. L., would not help him to seek a better life.[8]

The Freedmen's Bureau could not offer Violet Maples assistance. Most of its work was done by the end of 1868, and the agency folded in 1872. The Freedmen's Bureau could intervene when a dispute involved the fairness of formerly enslaved persons' contracts, which the bureau oversaw. For example, in February 1866, when Lucinda Jacoway complained to the bureau in Arkansas that William Bryant was demanding fifty dollars for her four-year-old girl, John Vetter, a bureau agent, instructed Bryant to return the child to her mother immediately. In *Stolen*

Childhood: Slave Youth in Nineteenth-Century America, Wilma King describes other mothers and fathers who made similar complaints, though the outcome of their requests is still unknown.[9] Chancellor J. F. Simmons, who decided *Maples v. Maples* in the local court, saw no reason to deprive Violet of custody. But Mississippi Supreme Court judge Jonathan Tarbell reversed the lower court decision and denied Violet's appeal. Tarbell based his decision giving custody to Ambrick on the highest ethical motives used often by supposedly well-intentioned Union officials. In accepting Violet's unfitness morally and economically, he concluded, "From the evidence it is better for the boy where he is, than with his mother, who has no home to take him to."[10] This case is one, where, Tarbell said, "to use a common expression, 'it would be better to let well enough alone.'"

Violet could have thought she had a good chance to win in the appeals court and keep custody of Boss. Not only did Republican Reconstruction still control when the case was decided, Tarbell was one of the Northern carpetbaggers who had fought in the Civil War and stayed on during Reconstruction. After military service, he worked in the Freedmen's Bureau, trying to enforce contracts to get planters to give freed people justice, which included pay for their labor and protection from ex-Confederates taking their children. He was appointed by Reconstruction Republicans to the highest court in Mississippi for a six-year term in 1868.

But the view of ex-Confederate Democratic politicians in the state that Tarbell was a reasonable moderate was reflected in his opinion. He did not even acknowledge the fragility of relationships between black fathers and mothers during slavery when marriage was prohibited, and how husbands and wives and children were often separated by sale or death. He did not recognize Violet's hopes for the future of her family. More curiously, he did not question the influence and interests of those who paid for this appeal. He based his decision on Violet's precarious status, not her humanity.

Seven years after the appeal was decided, Violet; her son Henry, now age eight; a daughter, Lucy, age four; and Violet's two brothers, Silas and Prince, now ages nineteen and seventeen, respectively, still lived together at the Bridgeforths. She, at age forty-five, was labeled a housekeeper rather than a cook, as in the case that decided their fate. The two older boys were laborers. Boss was an adult but still in Mississippi.

What happened to the Maples was not only a stealing of black labor but the trauma of the inability to make choices, manifested in ways that have been a largely overlooked source of persistent inequality, and trauma over a loss of agency for so many black people. The result is a missed accounting of the role the trafficking of black children's labor played in shaping not just the economic options but the minds and souls of black families.[11]

Violet Maples and her descendants experienced family breakup and economic deprivation intergenerationally. Violet, her children, and brothers labored for the Bridgeforths and neighboring planters. Hired out at first to various local white farmers, Boss eventually became a small land-owning farmer himself. His brother Tom joined him and stayed nearby as they grew families. Tom became a tenant farmer, never an owner like Boss. Boss settled in Plum Point and, in 1882, married about sixteen-year-old Lizzie from the neighboring Duncan family. She disappears from the census after 1880 and perhaps passed away, because Boss remarried, and Lizzie's mother, Clory, and other family members remained in the neighborhood. Boss and several other black men in the neighborhood tried to exercise a right to vote but, like others elsewhere, were denied for "unexplained reasons."[12]

Boss's second marriage, in 1886, was to Lou Jarvis. In the 1900 US Census, when he was thirty-nine and she was thirty-eight, they still lived in Plum Point along with Lou's thirteen-year-old niece Susanna Jarvis. Lou had three children before she married Boss, but only one was alive and was not living with Boss and Lou. They still lacked education, reporting in the census as late as 1900, as in earlier censuses, that no one in the household could read or write. After Lou died, sometime before 1910, Boss married Carrie Strickland.[13]

Boss Maples, as the son of the white planter William Maples and Violet, was light enough so that in subsequent censuses these children from his marriage with Carrie were sometimes listed as black and other times as "mulatto." For example, in the 1920 census, Boss, age sixty-five; sons Joe, ten; Boss Jr., seven; and Thomas, one and a half, are "mulattoes." His wife, Carrie, thirty-eight, is "black."[14]

In the 1930 US Census, Boss was seventy-five; his wife Carrie was forty-eight; children were Joe, twenty; Boss, seventeen; and Thomas, twelve; Jordan (Judge) was nine. Judge's World War II draft registration card recorded 1918 as the year of his birth. He therefore would have been twenty-two in 1940. Boss was still a farmer, and the family were farm laborers.

With the advent of the automobile, Boss's two eldest sons, Joe and Boss Jr., briefly held jobs as factory workers in Memphis, about twenty miles away, one at the Firestone Tire Company and the other at Fisher Body Works. Joe died on December 20, 1939, of undetermined causes. He worked at Fisher and was married to Julia. In 1940, Thomas who was twenty-two, lived at 1097 Roosevelt in Memphis.[15]

Joe Bridgeforth, who was fifteen or sixteen at the time he followed Boss to Mississippi, also permanently resided in Plum Point. The two likely cousins both lived in Beat District 2 and farmed along with their wives and children. Joe married one of Violet Maples's sisters, Nancy, who was living in Plum Point with Ambrick, her father. She was one year older than Joe. Whatever tensions lingered from Violet's loss of Boss, they named one of their babies Ambrick. By 1900, Joe, like Boss, owned his house and farmland. In 1903, he was hired and paid $5.80 by the county supervisors for repairing a bridge.[16]

Joe and Nancy Bridgforth still lived at Beat 2 in 1940 when he was eighty-two and she was eighty-one. He had managed with the labor of family members to purchase some land to leave to his heirs. When he died, in 1941, his will indicated that he owned eighty-three acres, about two parcels of forty acres, given to his wife, and upon her death to his two daughters, Vandella and Minnie Payne, and their children and grandchildren. The land would then be divided among their children, including daughter Mary Jones, sons Joe Bridgeforth Jr. and Louis, and Joe Bridge-forth's grandchildren, Melvin Parker, Nancy May Johnson, and his daughter Caroline Saulsberry's children.[17]

In the 1940 US Census, Joe was described as an "unpaid family worker" on the land he owned and lived on. His son Joe (Alex), married to Susie Bridgeforth, died of bronchial pneumonia in 1951 in Memphis at age sixty-one. Amanda Bridgeforth, at that address, 798 Ida Place in Memphis, reported his death. His usual occupation was common labor and farming.

Boss and Joe, who were either friends or cousins, remained working-class farmers throughout their lives and their descendants remained working-class laborers, including domestic servants and factory workers. They managed to own their homes eventually, and Joe left some land to be divided among his heirs.[18] Joe and Boss and their children stayed near each other and helped each other keep a strong and close family structure though they were ordinary working-class people. They had meager economic resources but strong family relationships.

Joe and his family's prospects and economic futures most resembled that of Boss, though Joe was most likely R. L. Bridge-forth's son. R. L. kept insisting on having Joe come back to his plantation but took no legal action to force him. R. L. wanted Joe to return to Limestone, but he offered no incentives and tried to entice him back to labor on the farm for free.

R. L. Bridgforth had the financial ability to help anyone he chose, including Joe. He had thirteen slaves in the 1860 US Census, the last taken before the Civil War, eight males, one of whom could have been Joe, and five females, three of whom were of childbearing age. Based on R. L.'s probate documents and reports upon his death, in 1894, he left an estate of legacies and other property of about $400,000 to be administered in the years after his death. Even with the fluctuations in the economy, this was a sizeable sum at the time.[19]

As an aside, R. L.'s son John, whom he sent to Mississippi to bring back Boss and Joe, successfully filed a false claim for $375 with the Southern Claims Commission in December 1874 for aiding the Union. He wanted reimbursement because three of his horses had been taken in the first years of the war. In the claim, he reported being in Kentucky during the war. His Confederate gravestone shows his service in Company F, Ninth Regiment, Alabama Infantry, and the correct year of birth in 1847, along with his death in 1913, as recorded in the official Alabama Death Index.[20]

Tom Maples, also the son of William Maples and an unknown mother, and therefore Boss's stepbrother, lived in DeSoto County with Boss and Lou and was a day laborer; he lived near Boss thereafter.[21]

Among the Maples' descendants, Tom Maples's grandchildren, exceptionally among those who litigated the apprenticeship cases, eventually became middle class through migration, education, and politics. Clemmie, who was the daughter of Tom Maples, a half brother of Boss Maples, married Herbert Dixon, a son of local farmers who had also been enslaved. They moved from Mississippi, first to Kentucky. There, Herbert, who, like others in the extended Dixon-Maples family and other freed people, had only what amounted to a second-grade education, worked in the West Kentucky Coal Company mines in Earlington. The coal companies, like other employers, recruited heavily in the South, providing train tickets for those who accepted offers of employment. Earlington is where their seven children, including Gloria Dixon Taylor (1941–1996), the youngest, were born.

Herbert Dixon Taylor who married Clemmie Maples and migrated north from Mississippi

By 1950, Herbert Dixon discovered he had pneumoconiosis, black lung disease, from working in the mines. He operated a restaurant for a time. The federal government did not establish the Black Lung Program for those suffering the disability until 1969.[22]

As the mines became depleted, the Dixons, like other migrants, moved on. The Dixons went to Chicago hoping for better opportunities, where some of the older children did factory work. Herbert continued to work at casual laborer jobs. Gloria, despite the odds, managed to attend the Farragut School on the west side, apparently regarded as one of the better high schools in the city.

After Gloria Dixon married Charles Lamond Taylor in 1969, she worked in a Zenith factory, and he did electrical repairs for the public housing agency. They moved about twenty miles away, to Harvey, in 1972, which was an upgrade over the disreputable housing, with bugs, tenants shooting rats, and other problems in Chicago, and seemed relatively prosperous.[23]

Harvey, about six miles square, was founded in 1891 by Turlington W. Harvey, a close associate of Dwight Moody, the founder of the Moody Bible Institute, in Chicago. Harvey was originally intended as a model town for Christian values and was one of the Temperance Towns. It was closely modeled after the company town of Pullman, which eventually was annexed into the city of Chicago.

Harvey had its greatest growth in the post–World War II years, when it was home to the Buda Engine Company, which was acquired by Allis-Chalmers in 1953. The city reached its peak population in 1980. By this time, it was beginning to suffer losses in jobs and population through the restructuring of steel and similar industries. A major shopping area, the Dixie Square Mall closed in November 1978.

In the 2000s and 2010s, Mayor Eric Kellogg attempted to boost Harvey's economy, with little success. Kellogg offered developers millions of dollars in incentives to revive the long-vacant Dixie Square Mall, but trends in retail adversely affected malls around the country. The city granted a developer $10 million in incentives to redevelop the Chicago Park Hotel, but he abandoned the project before completion, leaving the building gutted. In February 2018, Harvey became the first city in Illinois to have its revenue garnished by the state to fund the city's pension liabilities. The city laid off employees to deal with the problem.

After moving to Harvey, Gloria Dixon Taylor became very active in her church, Bethlehem Temple Missionary Baptist, and the community. In the 1970s, as Harvey struggled with economic decline, she was first elected as park commissioner in 1977. After becoming aware of how youngsters kept gathering under the tree outside their house where they at least had shade, she was determined to find ways to remedy the absence of activities or play places for the community's youth. She organized support that led to the building of a community park. She also consistently supported youth academic programs. In 1991, Gloria Dixon Taylor became the first black alderwoman for the Third Ward and the first to serve on the city council. For over twenty years she worked the midnight shift in the administrative office at

Gloria Dixon Taylor, Maples' slaves descendant, Harvey, Illinois, public official and community organizer

Joliet Correctional Center, driving back and forth from Harvey. Gloria Dixon Taylor died in 1996, survived by her husband; daughter Theresa, born in 1966; and son Clifford, born in 1971.

Gloria Dixon Taylor's daughter, Theresa, has with great determination devoted herself to serving the community with an emphasis on children. She founded and became the chief executive officer of the Gloria J. Taylor Foundation, dedicated to her mother's legacy. Her brother Clifford is credited as a cofounder and chief financial officer. As a child, she had been a TRIO program participant herself, and the TRIO programs are central to the foundation's work. These are federally funded educational opportunity outreach programs designed to motivate and support students from disadvantaged backgrounds to gain further education. Her son, Jovon, is director of operations for the foundation and associate director of the Upward Bound Program. Theresa is grooming her daughter Jayla to someday take over the foundation and its programs. Other family members, including her nephews Devon and Kevon Taylor and cousin James Dixon, also work at the foundation.

Theresa Dixon Taylor explains that she decided to gain as much education as possible so that she would be professionally efficient and effective in operating the foundation and its program. She earned a bachelor of arts degree in business administration from Governors State University, a master of science degree in human services and counseling from National Louis University in Chicago, and a doctor of education degree in child/youth and adolescence studies from Nova Southeastern University's Fischler Graduate School of Education and Human Services in Fort Lauderdale, Florida. She is a member of the American Counseling Association and co-chair of Illinois state senator Napoleon B. Harris III's Education Committee. Theresa also became an activist politician, serving as commissioner like her mother while running the Gloria Taylor Foundation and

Dr. Theresa Dixon Taylor, Chief Executive Officer of the Gloria J. Taylor Foundation, dedicated to her mother

its programs. She continued to serve on the commission and the Taylor programs into the 1990s.

In February 1996, after Theresa was elected the new board president, the commission appointed Angel Marzal, a Hispanic ancient history professor, to assume Gloria Taylor's position as commissioner until the expiration of her term in April 1997. Theresa said she supported the appointment, explaining that Hispanics were a growing population that had asked for more attention to their needs at a September meeting, including a permanent soccer practice field and more Spanish-speaking police dispatchers and officers.[24]

In June 1996, in a letter to the *Star*, Concerned Citizens of Harvey—Leslie Williams, Janice Grant, and Ronald Roberts—praised Dr. Theresa for being a grassroots politician and for keeping her word. She kept her promise to bring back a summer camp program, organized a Little League team, and took the children to a Chicago White Sox game, paying for tickets and food. She asked the board to approve a program that would help students who had to walk home unsupervised from school, as well as a recreation program for seniors. She, they noted, had done this while having a fulltime job and developing the Gloria Taylor Foundation to serve the community.[25]

In 1999, Dixon ran for alderman against incumbent John Arrington and lost narrowly. She raised funds locally at car washes, solicited collections, and engaged community organizations in helping to sustain the foundation. After it was well established, Dixon became a consultant for higher education institutions on mentoring and remediation though TRIO programs. For example, she served as director of the Prairie State College Talent Search Program in 2016; she also lectured at community colleges and helped to develop these programs at other institutions in the Chicago area.[26]

Gloria Taylor, and her daughter and siblings and descendants, moved higher up the economic ladder based on migration out of the South and the resilience some members of the family showed. But they were exceptional compared to some of the other descendants of slavery and apprenticeships who were parties in the state supreme court cases. They could not know exactly what their foreparents endured, or the trauma and deprivation they experienced, in slavery and afterwards, but the Dixon-Taylors, like other descendants of slaves, understand what it took to overcome the social and economic effects of that history.

CHAPTER 10

THE OTHER BRIDGEFORTHS

The contrast between the formerly enslaved who went to court to void forced apprenticeships and sometimes failed—those who experienced slavery by another name in convict leasing, inequitable share-cropping and tenant farming, and other abuses after Emancipation—who struggled to move ahead, and those who had better family treatment from their slave master relatives (in their multiple forms) is one explanation for how some black people and their descendants improved their economic status while others did not. Not every unaided poor family had the grit and circumstances of the Dixon-Taylors for example. The biracial child of a beneficent father slaveholder had resources unimaginable in contrast with the millions of poor formerly enslaved.

Consider the contrast between and the effect of how slave-owning brothers R. L. and James Bridgeforth treated their enslaved sons and how their families' lives were affected. We have only to consider R. L. Bridgeforth's non-relationship with son Joe Maples alongside James Bridgeforth's support of his enslaved "mulatto" son George. Joe, keeping close to Boss and Tom Maples, did fairly well economically, but nothing like the George Bridgeforths, whose former owner, his father, provided much more than the proverbially promised "forty acres and a mule."

When James Bridgeforth arrived in Limestone County in 1855, he built a log house on a rise overlooking Sugar Creek Bottom lands. It still exists and appears to be the only house in the county with a stairway leading directly off the front porch to upstairs. The house also has a façade embellished with wooden lentils, a glass transom, and sidelights.[1]

Upon the abolition of slavery through ratification of the Thirteenth Amendment, in December 1865, there was no need for running away or a lawsuit or the Freedmen's Bureau. Before twenty-three-year-old George could even plan leaving home, his father, James Bridgeforth, told him he was free and offered him financial resources and guarantees for future agricultural holdings and prosperity if he stayed. George stayed, and James Bridgeforth kept his promises and gradually helped George to develop a prosperous farming operation, the basis for his family's and descendants' wealth into the twenty-first century. Much like white antebellum slave owners who supported their concubines and slave children in addition to their white families, James gave his biracial son, George, financial help upon his emancipation. This enabled some newly free families to move from subsistence to opportunity.

By 1888, when only a few blacks owned forty acres or more and most black men worked as sharecroppers or wage laborers, when George's crops made a profit, he would buy more land, relying on his father for any additional funds or to facilitate a lien on future crops to make purchases. By 1910, George Bridgeforth owned about three hundred acres and was the largest black landowner in Limestone County.[2]

George benefited from his father's help and his own hard work and sound decisions. And the son in turn instilled the value of maintaining strong family ties and mutual support in his children, who passed it on intergenerationally. He could afford to make sure his sons were well educated and did so. Isaac (Ike) (1879–1968) attended Tuskegee Institute, returned home, and started a farm next to his father. The eldest son, George Ruffin Bridgeforth (1919–1996), perhaps named for George L. Ruffin, was the first black graduate of Harvard Law School in 1869, went to boarding school in Athens, then to Talladega College, and then to Amherst, graduating from Massachusetts Agricultural College in 1901. In 1902, he was hired to teach agriculture at Tuskegee, also assisting George Washington Carver, the director of agriculture. Soon Carver and George Ruffin Bridgeforth differed over how to manage the programs. Also, Carver's reputation and publicity about his work at Tuskegee might have been an irritant.[3]

George Ruffin Bridgeforth took his knowledge of improving community farming home to Limestone County. Aided by his father and brothers, he bought land next to his father's property, on the Elk River, for $4,500 deeded to him, with his parents and brothers as part owners. In 1909, three months before final payment was due, Bridgeforth paid off the land in full.

The Bridgeforths were the only black farmers in Limestone County in 1910 with over 250 acres. George Ruffin then founded the Southern Small Farmland Company to encourage black land ownership of land and improved methods of farming done on a cooperative basis, to buy and sell land and to merchandise seed, fertilizers, farming utensils, and other articles needed by and of benefit to its members and the public in general. The idea of cooperative black farming to make landownership possible for poor black farmers had persisted since Civil War efforts to gain land and was emphasized by Booker T. Washington at Tuskegee during Ruffin's time there. He was president of the company, and major shareholders were members of the Bridgeforth family.[4]

At first, black tenant farmers were reluctant about buying land for farming, thinking it was illegal for blacks to become owners. But then they asked some whites if it was legal for them to own land, farm animals, and pay taxes and were told it was all right.[5] They then bought land from the Southern Small Farmland Company. As a result, by the time of the last transaction recorded by the Southern Small Farmland Company, in 1913, blacks who had never owned land became part of the all-black community George Ruffin Bridgeforth called Beulahland. He took the name from Beulah, referred to in the Book of Isaiah as the "earthly paradise" to which the Israelites would return. The song "Beulah Land" was written in 1876 by Edgar Stites became a message of hope for a brighter future among blacks in Alabama, where the Bridgeforths resided, and across the country. Over the years, Beulahland has been referred to in various hymns and other works and was popularized by the black nationalist Reverend Albert Cleage in the late 1960's and '70s.[6]

When the last of the formerly enslaved Bridgeforths died in the early 1920s, Jennie in February 1922 and George in September 1923, the family was quite prosperous. With the help of his white father, James Bridgeforth, and their own efforts, they owned some of the most fertile land in Limestone County. Two of their sons had graduated from college, one becoming a college professor and administrator; the other, a successful farmer. Among their other children were landowners in the all-black community of Beulahland.

After leaving Tuskegee in 1918, George Ruffin Bridgeforth became head of Kansas Vocational College in Topeka, and from there an administrator at Tennessee Agriculture and Industrial College in Nashville. He stayed in close contact with his family and often visited the community. He returned to Limestone County in 1933, lived in Athens, and frequently visited his farm and family in Beulahland.[7]

George Ruffin Bridgeforth gave the community land and applied for a grant from the Rosenwald Fund to build an elementary school. The residents gave timber and labor, collected funds to pay teachers' salaries, and provided the teachers room and board. For further education, the nearest black high school was in Athens, 267 miles away.[8]

Franklin D. Roosevelt's New Deal damaged the lives of both black and white Southern tenant farmers, because the policies favored owners. Landowners in Beulahland did not apply for and did not receive public relief, but they acquired loans at the lowered interest rates made available by the Federal Land Bank. When the federal government, in 1933, began paying farm owners $7 to $10 an acre not to plant cotton, this also helped some Beulahland owners.[9]

Sadly, the Tennessee Valley Authority's decision to build Wheeler Dam and Reservoir on the Tennessee River brought bigger trouble to Beulahland and black farmers. TVA had the laudable purposes of better flood and erosion control and the production of electricity, thus modernizing the local river communities. But TVA land acquisition, beginning in 1934, forced families to relocate, including some from Beulahland.

The white TVA administrators had for the first time to work with a large black population. In addition, these black farmers were doing well compared to non-Beulahland farmers. While TVA noted that the "ability to get along on its cash crop, cotton, had made livestock relatively scarce" in the area, this did not apply to the Beulahland farmers. Most of them owned at least one or two mules, hogs, and poultry. Cows, which were particularly scarce in the Wheeler area, were their favored animal even among tenants. Each family had at least one cow, and several owned four or five.

During the relocation, while George Ruffin Bridgeforth lost 365 acres to TVA, he still owned remaining acreage, and his brothers and three other owners purchased tracts from him. Several of the families simply moved their homes onto partial tracts, which they were able to buy and keep.

Land values in the area increased when the larger white landowners, expecting developers to move in because of the reservoir, refused to sell any land. The land that the relocated farmers had been able to buy was hillier and not as fertile as the land that had been taken by TVA.

While TVA promised assistance in finding land of equal value, among all the families that relocated, only Bascom Bridgeforth's family received any help from the agency. He refused to move, for the $17.50 an acre they offered. He insisted he had hired a lawyer to bring suit and resisted until they negotiated with him and offered $50 an acre—the same amount white farmers received.

Beginning in 1934, the Bridgeforths kept trying to get TVA approval for projects to benefit the community without success. At first, they got a sympathetic ear, if not positive effort, in response. However, officials who ran the agency after 1939 didn't want to offend local whites. Officials, based in Knoxville, never had direct contact with Bridgeforth or the black community, and were suspicious of the Bridgeforths.[10] The representatives of government that might have helped, and were in fact tasked to help, refuse assistance because of representatives couldn't believe that George Ruffin Bridgeforth wanted progress for the community instead of just profits.

In 1938, TVA turned over the project to the local whites running the Limestone County Soil Conservation District, who let white landowners take over the cotton-field preparation work formerly done by black farmers. They justified this with the explanation that the whites had tractors that were more efficient while the black farmers still had mule-drawn equipment. Black farmers protested that they now were left with less profitable livestock and other crops to support their families and pay their taxes. George Ruffin Bridgeforth told the federal administrator that the reason was race discrimination.

But George Ruffin didn't just complain, and the Bridgeforths had financial resources. Within a year, both George and Bascom Bridgeforth purchased tractors and their farmwork became mechanized. They also began the county's first dairy operation.

George Ruffin organized the residents of Beulahland in cooperative gardening projects and taught management and farming practices to the young farmers. He also worked to get equal pay with white teachers for black teachers and for voter registration. He became one of the first blacks in the county to register to vote since the early 1900s, and he continued to encourage voter registration among blacks up until his death in 1954.

So, despite weather, the boll weevil, racist violence, an indifferent federal agriculture loan structure, and hostile local banks and businesses, the Bridgeforths kept strong family ties, encouraged mutual and community responsibility as they survived, led, and prospered in Limestone County. Help from their slave owner progenitor and ancestor and their own hard work undergirded the economic success of the family. If they had not had to contend with segregation and discrimination, perhaps they would have been even more prosperous.

Still, even when faced with challenges, the family's standing served as a form of protection. During Prohibition, Bascom had an encounter with the law when he was convicted of "making whiskey," which accounted for more arrests than any other violation in Limestone County and elsewhere at the time. He was ordered to serve only a minimum sentence, from February 1927 to May 1928, instead of the maximum, to November 1928.[11]

The family's prosperity and community reputation also protected two family members accused of more serious criminal
activity. Two of Isaac Bridgeforth's sons, George Bridgforth's
grandsons, who were brought up on felony charges, benefited
from their family's reputation and economic wherewithal.
Darden, for whom Darden Bridgeforth Enterprises, the family
company, was named, escaped severe punishment after he killed
a man with whom he had an argument. The other was William
Sousa Bridgeforth, who became a successful and wealthy pool
hall, café, and gambling enterprise businessman in Nashville,
Tennessee. He even bought the local black baseball team, and
he avoided conviction for tax evasion in the 1960s.

William "Sou" authored "The Brief Life and Grateful Times
of William Sou Bridgeforth," written in July 2001 and included
in his funeral program in 2004. The autobiography described
how "Sou," the first-born of Isaac and Ella Stuart Bridgeforth,
in Alabama, sent to live with his maternal grandparents, Mary
and Henry Stuart, after his mother died when he was six.

When he was eighteen, his mother's brother, his uncle Nick
Stuart, came to Athens and took him to Nashville. He taught
him his trade of bricklaying and encouraged him to be "tops" in
his field. He became an expert and financially successful. He laid
the black brick in front of the legendary segregated black Pearl
High School in 1936. He even won a competition with another
outstanding bricklayer, receiving an increase in his hourly pay
as a result.

In September 1929, Sou married Helen Mai King of Nashville in Williamson County. She was nineteen and her uncle,
Captain L. J. McLinn, was her witness. The 1940 US Census
reported them as divorced. When he was sixty-nine and she
was forty-eight, he married Katherine Dora Noble in Nashville
in 1976.

After his grandfather died in 1925, and his grandmother in 1927, their heirs eventually sold 280 acres of their land, and Sou inherited $420. He describes buying a decent suit to replace a too well-worn one and some new shoes, and with the $270 he had left, he opened a small pool room at Seventeenth Avenue North and Charlotte Street. A year later he moved the pool hall closer to downtown Charlotte, between Fourth and Fifth Avenues North. By 1936, he was able to open the New Era Club in a building upstairs at Charlotte Avenue between Fourth and Fifth Avenues. In 1941, the club was moved to Fourth Avenue North near Charlotte, where the Municipal Auditorium now stands. In 1955, he moved the club to Twelfth Avenue North and Charlotte Avenue. With the construction of the interstate in 1968, he described himself as "forced" to move the club to Eleventh and Charlotte.[12]

Sou proudly proclaimed that most leading black entertainers had played there, including Aretha Franklin and B. B. King. He was also delighted to have helped many aspiring local musicians get started. When Sou registered for the draft in 1940, he reported his age as thirty-three and that he worked for brick manufacturers and mason contractors Fulcher and Poyner.

Sou, explaining that he had always been a devotee of baseball, bought a black baseball team. He described playing as a young boy in Alabama and how his father Isaac's love of the game passed on to him. He claimed that as a pitcher and a catcher, he was labeled "Steel-Arm Red." In Nashville, he said, "I played with my team . . . the New Era Giants. We had many sell-out games in Hadley Park, and we were fierce competition." He gives credit to his business success for making it possible for him to "purchase and play with the Birmingham Black Barons," 1948–1954. As a proud member of the "Old Negro League," he also played amateur ball until he was forty-two.

All this, according to Sou, was done with his club profits, as he bought his first Negro League baseball team, the Baltimore Elite Giants, in the 1940s, then the Nashville Stars and the Birmingham Black Barons. But there was another side of the story that went unmentioned. In 1959, the federal government won a federal district court verdict for $5,000 cashing in a universal life insurance policy Sou had taken out with his then wife, Helen, as beneficiary in payment of unpaid taxes. There was no appeal. In 1961, the federal government filed a suit to sell some of Sou's property to pay off $52,608 in unpaid federal gambling and other taxes.[13]

In February 1964, Sou and other downtown club owners were accused of tax evasion by a federal grand jury. Some indictments were expected from a grand jury probe into alleged payoffs by eight club operators to local law enforcement officers. Sou and another owner, Mickey Kreitner of the Jolly Roger, had already been before the grand jury and were called back again. Bridgeforth left the jury room to consult with his attorneys three separate times.[14]

In 1965, the press reported that a federal judge ordered Sou to pay a debt owed to Mrs. Eva Komisar, who held a mortgage on a property he possessed and which the federal government sold to satisfy a tax claim. When the property at Twelfth and Charlotte was sold, the government claimed Sou owed $52,608 in unpaid taxes.[15]

In 1966, based on their possession of a federal wagering stamp, Sou and some white alleged offenders were accused of running the local numbers rackets. Though black locals insisted part of the defense strategy was to have relatives take the fall if anything seemed to lead to a conviction, the cases involving Sou dragged on, with the defense lawyers fending off any apparent resolution. Whatever the facts, he remained publicly acknowledged as a respected businessman and former baseball club owner until his death in 2004. (My brother Reverend Troy Merritt of Nashville, who has been acquainted with the local relatives, is quick to point out that if Sou hadn't faced exclusion because of his race, with his talent he probably could have been a wealthy financier on Wall Street and even more prosperous than he was.)[16]

In 1941, Isaac's son, Darden, at age twenty-six, at first seemed mired in deeper trouble than Sou. He was convicted and served jail time while awaiting trial and appeals for shooting and killing Flint Cain, a young black man, despite claiming self-defense. The press reported that as the Limestone County Negro Baptist Association was concluding its business on the afternoon of August 27, 1941, people panicked when they heard gunshots. Some drove quickly away, and others ran into the surrounding fields. Darden fired five times, hitting the twenty-five-year-old Cain. They had apparently been arguing that afternoon over some cigarettes.[17]

Darden claimed that Cain went into a field and returned with two bricks and threatened to kill him, whereupon he first fired a warning shot and then killed him with four other shots when Cain did not relent. Witnesses, however, said Cain had nothing in his hands and all of the shots were fired into his body. Sheriff's deputies arrested Darden a half hour later at his home near Tanner.

Judge David Lee Rosenau Jr., in the Municipal Court of Limestone County, held an all-day hearing before a crowded courtroom on the charges against Darden, described by the *Decatur Daily* on September 3, 1941, as a "representative of a prominent negro family of this county." The county solicitor, George Johnson, charged that the evidence showed the dispute occurred when Darden got out of a truck with a pistol in his hand and shot Cain after they argued over parking the truck. Darden's lawyers, R. B.

Patton and D. U. Patton of Athens, insisted that Cain menaced Darden with two bricks. Maxie Harris appeared as a defense witness to affirm the claim of self-defense and was charged with perjury and posted bond. Darden was ordered held without bond for grand jury disposition.

On November 13, 1941, the *Limestone Democrat* reported that after a two-day trial with dozens of witnesses, Darden was convicted with a punishment of twenty-five years. The grand jury set a hearing on his case of second-degree murder. Some witnesses pointed to Flint's record of having served time for shooting into a dwelling house, and Price Bridgeforth, Darden's twenty-two-year-old cousin, affirmed Darden's story of being threatened with rocks and found himself also charged with perjury all to no avail. The perjury charges were continued to 1945 and later continued probably because of military service.

After awaiting the outcome of his appeal in prison, Darden's conviction was reversed, and he was remanded for a new trial in December 1942. The opinion by Justice Virgil Bouldin, in which Chief Justice Lucien Gardner and Judges Arthur Foster and Thomas Lawson concurred, offered the rationale of "procedural difficulties."[18]

Not until October 4, 1945, did the Limestone County circuit court begin considering "old cases," including Darden's. On November 1, the *Alabama Courier* reported that he had served part of his twenty-five-year sentence before being released after the Alabama supreme court reversal and that this second trial took all day Tuesday and Wednesday until the jury was declared hopelessly hung.[19]

Darden was still free when on March 20, 1947, the *Courier* reported that the circuit court judge Newton B. Powell had set his case among several criminal cases for the term beginning on March 31. This time the indictment charged first-degree murder, with Darden's cousin Price Bridgeforth and Maxie Harris, who had testified in his case, facing charges of perjury.

On April 3, 1947, the *Courier* reported that Darden had been convicted of manslaughter with probation as the punishment with a hearing set April 19. Judge Powell, at a special probation hearing on April 20, announced Darden was "at liberty pending good behavior" and his sentence was five years. The perjury charges against his cousin Price and Maxie Harris were both dropped. The resolution of the charges against Darden and the others was helped by the Bridgeforth family prominence in the area.[20]

Thereafter, with the criminal charges behind him and probation as the final resolution, Darden Bridgeforth worked with his father, Ike, in the timber business and then returned to farming. Subsequently, he and six of his sons, who chose to follow him into agriculture, owned over 1,400 acres and rented another 5,100 acres.

Darden Industries was named after him, and his sons, Greg and Bill, began to run the company. Greg and Bill's older sister Doris in her seventies managed the office in the same small brick house where she had once lived with her twelve siblings. She recalled life in the early years, when they had the segregated one-room school she attended next to the family church and the segregated bathrooms and water fountains in neighboring towns.

Beulahland today numbers just a dozen houses, mostly owned by Bridgeforth relatives, many of whom still live in the community. Bill's sons, Kyle and Carlton, graduated from Morehouse College and worked in banking in New York before they came back to Beulahland in 2012. As of 2022, Carlton was a staff member on the US House Committee on Agriculture.

The success story of the George Bridgeforths provides a stark comparison with that of the black farmers fighting to keep their

land despite financial reverses represented by John Boyd, head
of the National Black Farmers Association. Boyd and his members express wariness about their relying on the Bridgeforths'
support on some important issues because the Bridgeforths' economic status seems more comparable to that of well-off white
farmers. Though the association won the *Pigford v. Glickman*
case in 1999, charging discrimination by the US Department of
Agriculture against black farmers, discrimination persists. One
example of the ongoing discrimination Boyd's group cites is the
failed promise of Section 1005, Emergency Relief for Farmers of
Color, of the American Rescue Plan (ARP), passed to alleviate
the Covid pandemic effects and signed into law by President Joe
Biden in 2021.

ARP included two provisions that seemed to provide needed
relief to black, Indigenous, and farmers of color. First, the bill
provided $4 billion in debt relief for certain USDA farm loans.
The program offered loan forgiveness to socially disadvantaged
farmers and ranchers (SDFRs), defined as those "belonging to
groups that have been subject to racial or ethnic prejudice."[21]
Shortly after, white farmers filed a lawsuit claiming reverse discrimination and tied up the $4 billion that was promised to
farmers of color. This lawsuit immediately stopped debt relief
from being distributed. The US Congress eliminated the provision altogether from the Inflation Reduction Act of 2022, passed
with only Democratic Party support. Boyd's group of farmers
have been trying unsuccessfully to get the Agriculture Department to give black farmers relief from imminent foreclosure in
the absence of the funds they expected to pay off crushing debt
of long standing. They point out that they have already shown
in court the effect of the Agriculture Department's failure to
give them available loans because of their race, forcing them to
borrow from private-sector banks.

As recently as the middle of 2023, the debt relief was still inaccessible, and black farmers and farmers of color were still being served foreclosure notices. In the Inflation Reduction Act, signed by President Biden on August 16, 2022, the Emergency Relief for Farmers of Color was repealed. New language now reads as "Assistance for Certain Farm Borrowers." The $4 billion in aid was reduced to $1.2 billion. With these changes, the debt relief is now accessible to the 95 percent of farmers who are white. Today, roughly 2 percent of farmers identify as black or mixed race compared to 14 percent a hundred years ago. For centuries, white farmers have been able to receive government relief without the barriers on local, state, and national levels that black farmers have faced.

John Boyd points out the drafters of the original bill aiding farmers of color included provisions making whole those *denied* USDA loans as a form of discrimination. The drafters knew from the reports done by the US Commission on Civil Rights, as well as from news reports over the years and the *Pigford* decision, that most poor black farmers never even applied for USDA loans after countless were turned down because of their race.[22]

Meanwhile, though the George Bridgeforth descendants had difficulty with the TVA and other issues, overall, their story is one of overcoming and success. They had strong family ties and financial resources. Joe Bridgeforth, Boss, and their descendants, and the other former enslaved in the apprenticeship cases, placed a similar emphasis on the importance of family sustaining each other, but they lacked sufficient resources for descendants generally to improve their economic status.

Callie Guy House (1861–1928), who helped gain reparations for formerly enslaved people, would say that there would be no reparations issue today if the land the formerly enslaved sought had been allocated as promised. Frederick Douglass, who supported reparations, would probably have agreed with her. What if Violet Maples could have kept her oldest son and, with the younger children, tried to make a better life? Imagine what might have been at least possible for so many of the formerly enslaved. Or imagine if Joe Bridgeforth's or Boss Maples's white fathers had provided for their biracial children as George Bridgeforth's father did.

And what could be their prospects today?

TWISTED TREES

Gulf-sized race-based gaps exist with respect to the health, wealth, and well-being of American citizens. They were created in the distant past but have indisputably been passed down to the present day through the generations. Every moment these gaps persist is a moment in which this great country falls short of actualizing one of its foundational principles—the "self-evident" truth that all of us are created equal.

—JUSTICE KETANJI BROWN JACKSON,
dissenting in *Students for Fair Admissions v. President and Fellows of Harvard College* and *Students for Fair Admissions v. University of North Carolina et al.* (2023)

B lack inequality seems intractable. Historically, it began in British North America long before Independence and the New Nation. At every stage of encounter with non-whites many Europeans chose white supremacy, whether by default or intentionally. In 1619, in exchanging the Africans landed in Jamestown on a pirate ship for provisions, white settlers made a decision affirming black inequality. Slavery and its legacy repeatedly excluded the choice of equality for blacks in decisions made in courts and legislatures.[1]

But we know that the end of legacy slavery did not end black inequality and white supremacy. This idea of tracing families affected by apprenticeships, consigning their children back to bondage after abolition, occurred to me long before the summer of 2023 Supreme Court affirmative action decision. In virtual discussions during the Covid pandemic and after with other scholars in the run-up to William Darity and Kirsten Mullen's publication of *From Here to Equality: Reparations for Black Americans in the Twenty-First Century*, I wondered how the children's experiences affected the perpetuation of inequality. They describe in their book:

> The formation of the republic provided a critical moment when blacks might have been granted freedom and admitted to full citizenship. The Civil War and the Reconstruction era each offered openings to produce a true democracy thoroughly inclusive of black Americans. Had the New Deal project and the GI Bill fully included blacks, the nation would have widened the window of opportunity to achieve an equitable future. Passage of civil rights legislation in the 1960s might have unlocked the door for America to eradicate racism. However, at none of these forks was the path to full justice taken.[2]

No wonder, given the circumstances, a poor, formerly enslaved woman, Callie Guy House saw the need for the Ex-Slave Mutual Relief, Bounty, and Pension Association in the late nineteenth century. The association, starting in 1898, organized mutual assistance and pressed the federal government unsuccessfully for pensions for the formerly enslaved. The federal government jailed House for "driving the negroes wild" by advocating reparations.[3]

Rendering reparative justice requires acknowledgment, redress, and closure. This book is about acknowledgment. It focuses on how keeping freed black children in uncompensated labor, by falsely claiming they had no parent who could care for them and therefore were apprentices, affected them. It is also about the unexplored effects on their relatives and specific descendants into the present. Acknowledging this history helps to explain why the perpetuation of "racial disparities in wealth, income, education, health, sentencing and incarceration, political participation, and subsequent opportunities to engage in American political and social life" need remedying.[4] It also helps to explain why resistance to the perpetuation of white supremacy and demands for reparative justice endure.

It also offers a response to the position that taking race into account as a remedy for racial disparities is unconstitutional, as reaffirmed by the Supreme Court in a 2023 higher education admissions case.[5] In dissent, Justice Ketanji Brown Jackson explained that

> those who demand that no one think about race (a classic pink-elephant paradox) refuse to see, much less solve for, the elephant in the room—the race-linked disparities that continue to impede achievement of our great Nation's full potential. Worse still, by insisting that obvious truths be ignored, they prevent our problem-solving institutions from directly addressing the real import and impact of "social racism" and "government-imposed racism," thereby deterring our collective progression toward becoming a society where race no longer matters. Today's gaps exist because that freedom was denied far longer than it was ever afforded.

The tracing of individual formerly enslaved families and their descendants shows specifically the kind of intergenerational harm they experienced that has been documented by scholars over the years. These apprenticeships were stolen child labor, not legal slavery, but the relationship and profit-making model was not much different. It was about former slave owners taking possession of the sons and daughters of newly freed blacks, exploiting the labor of the young. The resulting damage to families—literally and financially—has been a largely overlooked source of inequality and the diminished futures of many black people. The trafficking of black children's labor reduced the rewards of individual effort, thus constraining the future options of black families, but it also affected the psychological well-being of the abused.

Since marriages during slavery were not legally recognized, the court regarded any former slave child technically as an orphan who could therefore be routinely apprenticed. Local courts, at the behest of planters, apprenticed more than 2,500 black children in the South in the month after Emancipation. Like Boss Maples, whose grandfather claimed in court that he wanted to keep him, many of the children were simply hired out.

A large percentage of the 990,000 slaves in the 1860 population between the ages of ten and nineteen were likely apprenticed. The local state laws supposedly protected all children, but not black ones. This trafficking, called apprenticeships or hiring out by illegal custody claims, meant that parents like Violet and her child experienced not just the possibility of workers who could help the family but the disruption of personal ties. Like Violet, who lost Boss, and the people in other cases in this book, parents also had limited options with the younger, less-able-to-work children to support.

Planters pressured relatives, such as grandfather Ambrick Maples, to claim child custody so the child could be taken from parents. They also paid for appeals, to the highest state courts to overturn any Freedmen's Bureau or lower court decisions favorable to the child's relatives. Some relatives surreptitiously took their children and ran away with them. Others decided they had no alternative but to stay under the master's control, because they did not want to leave their children. Apprenticeships have received little attention by comparison with the other economic and political issues of the time, yet they provide one of the best examples of efforts to push blacks back into slavery.

After the Civil War, while white Southern family law decisions came gradually to align with those outside the South, the exploitation of black labor continued. Historian Peter Bardaglio explains that in Southern custody contests, pitting the parents against outsider parties between 1800 and 1865, outsiders, including relatives, prevailed in only 6 percent of cases. The Southern courts, like the Northern ones, used best interests of child, tender years, and ties developed between a custodial parent when an actual parent wanted the child back. About ten Southern cases involving formerly enslaved blacks, including *Maples v. Maples*, in state supreme courts have long been known to scholars, but researchers have not traced the parties and descendants, as far as possible, to determine their fate intergenerationally during and after Reconstruction into the late twentieth century.[6]

Imagine the impact on relatives, parents, and children who found each other after legal slavery ending up being separated from them by the so-called legal labor system. David Shalleck-Klein, one of the winners of the 2022 David Prize, which recognizes New York City–based change makers, has established the Family Justice Law Center to sue government agencies that separate parents from their children. He became interested in such a litigation center when family separation at the US-Mexico border became heavily publicized. He realized that the problem is not just at the US-Mexico border but also "here, in Harlem. It happens here in East New York. It happens in Williamsbridge, Bronx, and Jamaica, Queens, in the areas of the city that have the highest child poverty rates and the highest percentage of Black residents."[7]

Dorothy Roberts in *Torn Apart: How the Child Welfare System Destroys Black Families—and How Abolition Can Build a Safer World* (2022) describes the apprenticeship system as "another unacknowledged aspect of the history of child welfare. Many people know that states used the convict leasing system, Black codes, and prisons to subvert the Thirteenth Amendment and recapture Black labor. We hear less about the forced apprenticing of Black children."[8] Roberts sees these apprenticeships as "the origin of the formal child welfare system for Black families because it was court-imposed indenture of Black children back to their former enslavers by the thousands." In existing laws and in the apprenticeship laws enacted after abolition, courts could indenture black children to white people for their own good. "And many children were sent right back to the plantations and farms where they had been forced to work prior to the abolition of slavery," writes Roberts. They and their descendants, who largely worked in domestic service or farm labor could not even benefit from the Social Security retirement system enacted in 1935 because these two categories of labor were excluded until the 1950s.[9]

Beyond the plantation, nonagricultural employers also trafficked supposedly orphaned black children's labor after slavery. Not just adolescent boys but women and children worked in textile mills, for example, when they were not yet at the age and physical ability to pick enough cotton. In this way employees maximized the employer's productivity and profits. The policy results in the twentieth century are still with us.

One result is the misidentification of black youth, which has negative consequences. One example of this is the super-predator

theory, which the courts have continued to use to dispropor-
tionally convict and sentencing black youth. That theory was
disavowed by John Dilulio, who initially had advanced it in a
November 1995 cover story in the *Weekly Standard*, "The Coming of the Superpredators." But, in the meanwhile, it helped to
encourage Democratic Party officeholders' support of expanded
longer sentences and other tough-on-crime policies to ward off
the threat black youth seemingly posed. In overturning Keith
Belcher's sixty-year sentence for armed burglary and rape, the
Connecticut Supreme Court, in 2021, explained the historical
abuse of black children as a factor in the continued treatment
and misunderstanding of black youth. The court noted that in
the antebellum period, when "adolescence was being recognized
as a distinct developmental stage for white children, many Black
children remained enslaved and were viewed as subhuman."[10]
Kristin Henning, a law professor at Georgetown and the author
of *the Rage of Innocence: How America Criminalizes Black
Youth*, concluded that unlike with white children, "racism's logic
was that Black children didn't need to be protected; they needed
to be worked, disciplined, and punished."[11]

Researchers have confirmed also the negative effects of the
nutritional deprivation black children and adults suffered, not
just in slavery but in the post-emancipation labor system. They
see the resulting intergenerational transmission of inheritable
diseases as undermining the health and potential of blacks. At
first, Robert Fogel and Stanley Engermann's 1974 argument in
Time on the Cross, that the food consumption of enslaved blacks
was greater than that of whites, led to major public controversy
about whether slavery was a benign institution. The controversy
died down when studies proliferated affirming the nutritional
deprivation of enslaved and emancipated black mothers and
children, without regard to gender.[12]

For example, the relationship between inadequate nutrition and health conditions and high blood pressure, low-birth-weight infants, racial morbidity and mortality differences, and other deprivations have been well documented in recent years. These inadequacies began with black children during slavery and continued as they were exploited by the labor system and into adulthood, given the employment available, poverty, and missing or inadequate health care.[13]

Stanford economist Ran Abramitzky and Princeton economist Leah Boustan, and other researchers using FamilySearch, Ancestry.com, and other digitized materials, recently tracked whether immigrants who have come to the US since the Hart-Celler Act in 1965, many of whom are non-white but not black, are as upwardly mobile as European immigrants in the nineteenth and early twentieth centuries. Their findings turned out important information about the comparative fate of blacks who migrated out of the South after slavery. They found that "children of immigrants from Mexico and the Dominican Republic today are just as likely to move up from their parents' circumstances as were children of poor Swedes and Finns a hundred years ago."[14] They benefited from geographic mobility when their parents moved to where jobs were providing upward mobility for everyone, and they got jobs. They also eventually intermarried and gained English-language proficiency. But for blacks emerging from slavery, the perpetuation of social and economic deficits, legal discrimination, and exploitation persisted, and mobility out of the South came gradually. The Maples, Dixons, and Taylors discussed in chapter 9 exemplify the apprenticeship cases of blacks who migrated and achieved significant upward mobility.[15]

Some of the formerly enslaved discussed in this book and their descendants stayed in the South. Others left for the North in the Great Migration, which is divided into two parts, covering the

United States in both world wars. The first, between 1910 and 1940, saw black Southerners leave for Northern and Midwestern cities, including New York and Chicago, which included a few of the descendants in these cases. However, most of the Maples and other black descendants in Mississippi went North only to Memphis and further East, to what Luther Adams describes as "way up north in Louisville," in his book of the same name.[16]

In the second Great Migration, from 1940 to 1970, nearly four million Southern black migrants left the South for the North: Oakland, Los Angeles, and San Francisco, California; Portland, Oregon; and Seattle, Washington. Within twenty years of the end of World War II, three million more blacks had migrated across the country. Leah Boustan's *Competition in the Promised Land* points out that "instead of general upward mobility and black economic progress though migrants gained tremendously, more than doubling their earnings by moving North, they competed with existing black workers, limiting black–white wage convergence in Northern labor markets and slowing black economic growth." Furthermore, many white households responded to the black in-migration by relocating to the suburbs. Though white flight could have been motivated not only by neighborhood racial change but also by the desire on the part of white residents to avoid participating in the local public services and fiscal obligations to serve the increasing black population. Boustan concludes that "mobility as a remedy for structural discrimination did not have the same effect for blacks, the Promised Land turned out not to be so promising."[17]

One question that sometimes still emerges when reparations for slavery are discussed is why the slave owners and whites who were impoverished by the end of the institution should not be compensated. When Britain abolished the slave trade in 1807, slave traders were compensated. Slave owners were compensated in the District of Columbia when slavery was abolished in 1862. Slave owners in the British West Indies were compensated when slavery was abolished in 1833, and the slaves were apprenticed for a time in some colonies but were not compensated.[18]

Perhaps if slave owners had varied their investments and not relied on enslaving human beings for unpaid labor in perpetuity they would have been in better economic shape after abolition when it came. But they may have thought that slavery would persist or that given history if emancipation came, they would be compensated since it had happened before. It can be asked also what sense it would make to reward slave owners for fomenting the bloodiest war in United States history, killing people who were not slave owners in the North and the South over their insistence on keeping slave labor and expanding it, thus constricting opportunity for paid workers?

To the unrequited harm done to blacks during slavery and after, the use of apprenticeships to provide former slave owners with slave labor after the Thirteenth Amendment, must be added the experience of these children and families who fought, sometimes successfully and sometimes not, to prevent emancipated children from being pushed back to forced labor. Any consideration of reparative justice must take the suffering of these children and their families into account.

APPENDIX

The people I have written about in this book are not unknowable. We know some of the individuals who became enslaved after slavery, and we know who their immediate descendants were. Sometimes we can trace them until today; others we have only trails of their histories. Their families have been lost, stolen, or strayed and not acknowledged in records. I hope this appendix will give readers an opportunity to consider whether they may have connections to the children who were forced into apprenticeships after emancipation. I learned when I published *My Face Is Black Is True: Callie House and the Struggle for Ex-Slave Reparations* (2005) that even the names of the formerly enslaved who had the courage to sign petitions demanding reparations led some blacks to identify and then trace ancestors and community people about whom they had previously had no information. The appendix gives names, dates of birth, cause of death, employment, and other available details. This information can, of course, be used by scholars, students. and reparative justice activists. But a name, place, or situation could also lead a reader to others as we continue on the journey of excavating our history.

Detailed data was taken largely from Ancestry.com.

CHAPTER 1: *The Lost Children of Nathan and Jenney Cox, Cox v. Jones 40 Alabama 297 (1866)*

Nathan Cox (b. 1840–d. 1911?); w. Jenney (b. 1839–d. 1914?); children: Nathan F. (Felix), b. 1850; Henry, b. 1855; Daniel, b. 1859; Isham, b. 1860; and Matt, b. 1862 ("the boys apprenticed to serve until they are twenty-one years of age, and the girls until they are sixteen years of age."* Felix to serve up to five more years, Henry till 1871, Daniel 14 more years, Isham 15, to serve till age 21. Their parents, Nathan and Jenney Cox, lost their children to former master Francis Jones. The children eventually took the name Jones and left when apprenticeships were no longer feasible.

Nathan F. (Felix) (b. 1850), farmer; he is reported as married in 1877 in the 1900 US Census but no record of wife's name; children: Rolly (b. 1883).

Henry (b. 1855); w. Lizzie (b. 1871), children: Isham (b. 1887), age 13; daughter Nilla (b. 1884), age 16, both day laborers; Lula (b. 1894); Bunch (b. 1893); and Sweetbine (b. 1899).

Daniel (b. 1859), lived with Henry in 1880; farmhand.

Isham (b. 1860), lived with Henry in 1880; farmhand.

Matt (b. 1862–d. after 1950), age 87, still in Russell County widowed and unable to work; w. Lizzie (b. 1879–d. when she was 66, btw. 1940 and 1950).

CHAPTER 2: *Freeing Henry Comas, Comas v. Reddish, 35 Ga. 236 (1866)*

Jacob Comas (b. 1825–d. 1920) and common-law wife Easter; children: 5, including Henry (b. 1851); w. Jane (b. 1831);

Cox v. Jones 40 Alabama 297 (1866).

children: Charles (b. 1853), Jacob (b. 1855–d. 1930 in Alachua), Samuel (b. 1858), Peter (b. 1860), and Jane (b. 1863); all in farming.

Henry (b. 1851–d. 1926), employed as coachman; w. Jincey (b. 1852), laundress.

Jacob (b. 1855–d. 1930 in Alachua); w. ?; children: Jacob. (b. 1875), Jane (b. 1873).

CHAPTER 3: *The Rescue of Mary Cannon, Cannon v. Stuart 8 Del. 223 (Del. Super. Ct. 1866)*

James Cannon (b. 1847); w. Emeline (b. 1845); children: Mary (b. 1861–d. 1923), Francis (b. 1860), Prince (b. 1860), Charles (b. 1859), Joshua (b. 1864), Bell (b. 1871), Horace (b. 1874); none in school, all servants on Elisha Cannon's property in 1880.

Mary Cannon (b. 1861–d. 1923); h. John Vickers (d. 1929); children: Howard (b. 1883); Joshua (b. 1885); Minnie (b. 1887), did general housework in private homes; Mary E. (b. 1886) Ernest (b. 1891); Gertrude (b. 1897); Cutie (b. 1897); Willis (b. 1901); Kate (b. 1906); Edmunce (b. 1910); Elsie (b. 1916).

Prince Cannon (b. 1860); w. Mary Jane (b. 1884); worked always as farmer; children: Elias, Ida, Elwood, Bessie (b. 1896), Raymond (b. 1900), George (b. 1901), Lee (b. 1904).

Prince Cannon; w. Annie (b. 1878); children: infant daughter (b. 1910).

Charles Cannon, no info. after birth.

Joshua Cannon (b. 1864 [1867?]); w. Annie Wooten (b. 1870); self-employed farmer.

Bell Cannon (b. 1871), no info.

Horace Cannon (b. 1873/4–d. 1961) farmer, then chemical factory laborer, waterman in a hosing mill; w. Virginia Andrews; children: Laura, Frank James, and Emma; w. Ida Mae; children: Harry Leon, Alberta, Sina, Isaac Henry, Horace Leroy, and Edward.

Howard Vickers (b. 1883), farmer bought part of 27 acres of land from father and his brother George, which they had inherited from their mother, Fannie T. Burton Vickers (d. 1899), who bought it in 1891.

Joshua Vickers (b. 1885–d. 1922), farmer, bought part of 27 acres of land from father and his brother George, which they had inherited from their mother, Fannie T. Burton Vickers (d. 1899), who bought it in 1891. COD: described as chronic diffuse peritonitis, tuberculosis, or cancer.

Ernest Vickers (b. 1891), farmer, bought part of 27 acres of land from father and his brother George, which they had inherited from their mother, Fannie T. Burton Vickers (d. 1899), who bought it in 1891.

Mary E. Vickers (b. 1886); h. James Miller; children: Lincoln (b. 1911–d. 1961), Delia (b. 1918), Margaret, and Dorothy (b. abt. 1918–d. 1962).

Minnie did general housework in private homes.

Lincoln Miller (b. 1911–d. 1961); w. Anna Belle Farrin Miller; COD: cardiac arrhythmias due to congestive heart failure due to hypertensive cardiovascular disease.

Delia Miller (Byrd) (b. 1918–d. 1964); COD: enlarged heart, diabetes, mitral insufficiency, and rheumatic heart disease.

Employed as domestic worker; h. H. Leon Byrd; children: Bernice (b. 1932–d. 2006).

Margaret Miller (b. 1915–d. 1994), employed with railroad.

Dorothy Miller (b. abt. 1918–d. 1962); COD: hemorrhage and hypertension; employed as housework; h. William Purnell; children: Violet Phyllis Purnell.

Gertrude Vickers (b. 1897); h. Herman Hall; children: Mary Stewart (b. 1911–d. 1951), Delia (b. 1913); Herman Jr. (b. 1915–d. 1978).

Mary Hall Stewart (b. 1911–d. 1951); h. Edgar Stewart (b. 1912); employed as butcher.

Delia Hall (b. 1913).

Herman Hall Jr. (b. 1915–d. 1978).

CHAPTER 4: *The Emancipation of Eliza and Harriet Ambrose, Ambrose 61 N.C. 91 (1867)*

Hepsey Saunders (b. abt. 1843); h. Wiley Ambrose (b. abt. 1843); stepfather Hepsey's children: John Allen (b. 1862), Harriet (spelled Harriett in US Census) Ambrose (b. abt. 1851), Eliza Ambrose (b. abt. 1853).

Harriet Ambrose (b. abt. 1851); 1870, lived Onslow County, NC, with and worked for black farm family; h. Henry Hewitt (b. 1850–d. 1910) 1872; farm laborer nearby white farm family. By 1880, when she was 29 and he was 30, they had three boys: James, b. 1873), drayman; Henry (b. 1876) became a carpenter; m. Easter T. Kornegay in 1898 (b. 1876); and Frank (b. 1878). Father Henry remained a farm laborer, and Harriet was keeping house. Additional children: David (b. 1880), carpenter; Carrie (b. 1840), "nurse"; Alice (b. 1880); Mary (b. 1891); Calvin (b. 1893); and Daniel (b. 1895).

James Hewitt (b. 1873–d. 1929); COD: bronchial pneumonia and bronchitis; drayman, laborer; w. Mary (b.–d. bef 1909?), w. Alice Yancey (b. 1909?); lived with David in 1920.

Henry Hewitt (b. 1876), carpenter; w. Easter T. Kornegay (b. 1876); child: Jesse (b. 1898).

Frank Hewitt (b. 1878).

David Hewitt (b. 1880), carpenter; w. Edith Williams (b. abt. 1885–d. 1958) in Paterson, NJ; farmer owning home; 1920, James and his wife lived with him: 1930, Harriet widowed lived with him and his daughter Maria, age 29; at age 59, in 1939, David lived in Albert Daniels's lodging house at 87 W. 119th St. in New York City. He had a 4th-grade education and was a home builder in the contractor industry.

Carrie Hewitt (b. 1884); h. William O'Bryan (b. 1879–d. bef. 1920); children: William (b. 1908), rented house and lodger, employed as cook in household; remarried Mrs. Carrie O'Bryan May; lived at 120 W. 135th St. in New York in 1942.

Alice Hewitt (b. 1888–d. 1948), lived at 120 W. 135th St., New York; COD: cerebral apoplexy.

Mary Hewitt (b. 1891 or 1893); h. Albert Green (b. 1893); cook and mess sgt. WWI; postwar, millwright at an oil factory in New Bern, NC; divorced 1961. Green married Sadie Smith Desbrew in 1962; private, 15th Infantry, WWI.

Calvin Hewitt (b. 1893–d. 1978); w. Bessie Mack; moved to New Rochelle, NY, 1913; employed as waiter, pullman porter, and factory worker.

Daniel Hewitt (b. 1895); w. Amanda Bynum (b. 1897).

Eliza Ambrose (b. abt. 1853), laborer in fish factory; h. Jim Taylor (b. ?–d bef. 1910); children: Pauline (b. 1877–d. 1934).

Pauline Ambrose Bell (b. 1877–d. 1934); COD: cardio mitral valve problem with asthma as a contributory factor; could not read or write; h. Ezekiel Bell (b. 1874–d. 1941), could read and write; employed as laborer, tenant farmer; children: Emma (b. 1898), Phillis (b. 1901), James (b. 1902), Harold (b. 1905), Mary Liza (b. 1908), Homer (b. 1909); also Marie (b. 1901–d. 1970?); COD: stroke, cardiovascular event.

Emma Lee Bell Murrell (b. 1898–d. 1963); COD: chronic nephritis bronchial pneumonia, cerebral hemorrhage cerebral hypertension and diabetes); h. Christopher Columbus Murrell (b. 1888–d. 1965); COD: arteriosclerosis heart disease a farm laborer; children: Rosa (b. 1919), Columbus (b. 1920), Pauline (b. 1922); children: Caretta (b. 1925), Joe Nathan (b. 1928), Willie (b. 1931), McCline (b. 1933), John (b. 1936), Levi (b. 1938), Charles (b. 1939), Winston Churchill (b. 1942).

Emma Lee Bell Murrell & Christopher Columbus Murrell's children's children:

Rosa (b. 1919), 4th-grade education; h. Elisha Murray Jr. (b. 1917–d. 1959).

Columbus Jr. (b. 1920–d. 2014), could not read or write; w. Maggie Mae Taylor (b. 1922–d. 2005); children: Vita (b. 1938), Pearle (b. 1947), and Aron (b. 1949?); children: Tammy Murrell; Verdell Burns (b. 1950); Pearlie Harkley (b. 1946), at 16 married Richard Harkley in 1963, divorced 1988.

Pauline (b. 1922–d. 2008), finished fifth grade, never married, lived with parents; child: Curtis Murrell (b. 1946).

Caretta (b. 1925); h. Clifton Smith (b. 1925); child: Archard (b. 1950–d. 1950).

Joe Nathan (b. 1928–d. 2008); w. Lillie Mae Murray (b. 1929–d. 2022); children: Loretta (b. 1946), Nancy (b. 1948). Loretta married Arizona Jones in 1967 when she was 21 and he was 25.

Willie (b. 1931–d. 1985), worked on farm; w. Loretta Murray (b. 1930–d. 2004); 11th-grade education.

McCline (b. 1932); w. Thelma (b. 1931–d. 1989).

John (b. 1936–d. 1987); w. Vivian (b. 1940–d. 1999).

Levi (b. 1938); w. Menonia Foster (b. 1906?–d. 1962), worked in a tobacco factory in Winston-Salem; COD: coronary occlusion.

Charles Allen (b. 1939); w. Ruby Nell Murray (b. 1947).

Winston Churchill (b. 1942); w. Rosetta Murray (b. 1946).

Phillis Bell (b. 1901); h. O'Hara Pritchett (b. 1896) m. 1918.

James Henry Bell (b. 1902), registered for draft WW II 1941; was in Norfolk working for Virginia Ice and Freezing Co.; living with Mrs. Kathryn Bell, address 243 Suffolk St. Catherine was James Bell's wife. 1950 census.

Joseph Allen Bell (b. 1906–d. 1982), Morehead, Carteret County, NC; farmhand, Morehead; by 1930 worked in fish factory in his 40s; w. Margaret Luella (b. 1907–d. 1960); COD: acute cardiac decomposition, hypertensive heart disease.

Harold Bell (b. 1905), w. Mary J. Collins in 1925 in Morehead City. She was 17 and he was 19.

Mary Liza Bell (b. 1908), in 1930 she was a laundress still single, living with parents.

Homer Bell (b. 1909–d. 1988), in 1940 he owned a home, if rented $25 a month; his wife, Lucinda (b. 1911–d. 1985); 2 daughters: Ada Bell, 7, and Ester, 4. In 1950, Ely, 19; Donald, 15; Ester, 17; and Ada, 15, lived with them, and Homer worked at a fish factory. He registered for the WWII draft. Lucinda was a maid in a government agency. Homer died in 1988.

Marie (b. 1901–d. 1970?), COD: stroke-cardiovascular event.

Rosana Bell (b. 1912–d. 1964), ill with hypertension and diabetes; COD: cerebral hemorrhage; café cook; h. Fred Ernul (b. 1909–d. 1975); 4th-grade education; employed as car mechanic; child: Grace (b. 1930).

Haywood Bell (b. 1915–d. 1986), registered for the WWII draft; w. Thelma Fuller (b. 1917–d. 2003).

Bessie Bell (b. 1917).

Burnes Bell (b. 1922–d. 1992); w. Margaret Grace Jones (b. 1925–d. 2005); grammar school education; unskilled construction work; WWII military service.

Daisy Beatrice Bell (b. 1924–d. 1926); COD: bronchial pneumonia.

Marie (b. 1901–d. 1970?); h. Eunice Jackson (b. 1899); COD: stroke-cardiovascular event.

Marie Bell Jackson (b. 1901–d. 1970), worked at canning factory; h. Eunice Jackson (b. 1899)

CHAPTER 5: *Fighting for the Sons of Samuel and Oliver Adams, Samuel Adams v. William H. Adams 36 Ga. 236 (1867) and Adams v. McKay, 36 Ga. 440 (1867)*

Samuel Adams (b. 1835); children: Tucker (b. 1854), Francis (b. 1855), and Zachariah (b. 1856).

Tucker Adams (b. 1854); w. Patsy Dancy in 1877; in 1870, employed as fieldhand.

Zach Adams (b. 1856); w. Rebecca Adams (b. 1873); children: Simeon Adams (b. 1895), Owen Adams (b. 1896), Anice Adams (b. 1898), Wiley (b. 1900), Louisa (b. 1903), Nick (b. 1906), Baby Boy (b. 1909). Zach owned a farm with a mortgage. Zach reportedly could read and write, but no one else in the household could. Their daughter, Anice, married Milford Adison. She was a 41-year-old domestic who died September 9, 1929, in Carroll County having convulsions and then giving birth. They called the doctor; "he never came."*

Oliver Adams (b. 1831), w. Maxey (b. 1830); children: Jesse Morris (b. 1853); Harriet (b. 1854); Adams (b. 1855–d. 1930), COD: apoplexy, right side; Toss (b. 1856); Peter (b. 1860).

Jessie Morris (b. 1853); w. Maria (Mira); children: Susan (b. 1887), Josephine (b. 1890); employed as cab or hack driver, Macon, GA.

---

*Anice's death certificate: Georgia, US, Death Records, 1914–1940; Anice Anderson, Georgia State Board of Health, State File No. 26010; father Zach Adams; COD: "Child birth after Convulsions Dr. Called but never came."

Susan Morris (b. 1887); employed as public school teacher, h. Charles Lucas, insurance agent (b.?–d. bef. 1940); Susan widowed, lived with Lucas relatives on farm in Wilcox, Georgia. By 1950, she lived in Lake Florida with "negro" family: Robert Solomon, a "grove hand"; his wife, Mary; and their children, and is described as mother-in-law, employed as housekeeper for a private family.

Josephine Morris (b. 1890–d. 1955); h. Daniel Walker (b. ?); employed as private family chauffeur; children: Daniel (b. 1924), Josephine (b. 1925).

Daniel Walker (b. 1921–d. 2007); w. Johnella Earlene Charlton (b. 1922–d. 2013), in Roanoke, VA, where she was a clerk for the War Department; child: Daniel (b. 1947).

Josephine Walker (b. 1925); w. Alan Walton, a Veterans Administration clerk in the 1950 census; at that time she was a secretary in the Washington, DC, public schools. They had one daughter, Beverly, who was five in 1950.

CHAPTER 6: *The Case of Sarah Lacy, Timmins v. Lacy 30 Tex. 115 (1867)*

Harry Pope (b. ?); w. Sarah; children: Elkin (b. 1849), Chuff (b. 1866), and Leney (b. ?).

Moses Lacy (b. 1825); w. Sarah; stepfather to children: Elkin (b. 1849), Chuff (b. 1856), and Leney; w. Emiline (b. 1839); children: William (b. 1871), Cresanna (b. 1878).

Chuff aka Bush (b. 1856); w. Mary Dennis (b. 1872); children: daughters Nancy (b. 1887), Jimmie (b. 1889), Katie (b. 1891), Icie (b. 1894), Sallie (b. 1898–d. 1941); COD: pulmonary tuberculosis and contributing diabetes over 12 yrs. in state hospital; employed as housekeeper; and sons

Charles (b. 1895–d. 1870), COD: acute renal shutdown and anuria, chronic diabetes; and Walter (b. 1899); w. Anna Seynall (b. 1877).

(In 1930, a Leona Lacy was an "inmate" in Central State Hospital for the "feeble-minded" in Nashville; there were 45 other Negro inmates, including males and females, in the facility, according to the 1930 US Census.)

Harry Pope (b. 1824); w. Rachel Pope (b. 1845); children: Harriet (spelled Harriett in census) (b. 1864), Caroline (b. 1865), Green (b. 1868–d. 1972), and Rosana (b. 1870), Pope (b. female).

Rachel Pope (b. 1845); h. James Thacker (b. 1855); children: Rosanna (b. 1870), Green (b. 1868), and Harriet (b. 1864), and 4 of Thacker's children.

Green (b. 1868–d. 1938), owned a farm free and clear and was still farming in 1920; COD: a cerebral hemorrhage with paralysis; w. Sallie (d. 1918); children: George (b. 1907), Kayley (b. 1909), and a daughter Sylvester (b. 1909); COD: don't know, possibly acute indigestion" and "never treated disease" as "contributory," children: Gester (b. 1906–d. 1976); COD: cardiac arrhythmia and congestive heart failure); Ragion (b. 1912).

Gester (b. 1906–d. 1976); w. Pertha Braley (b. 1901–d. 1977) in 1973; farm laborer, "grammar school" education, imprisoned December 1908, 2 years along with Herbert Pope and Bud Morgan, fellow farm laborers, for 1 of 5 hog theft convictions in 1908, all black. There were 5 hog thefts, all by black farm laborers, listed on one page of the Texas convict register in 1908. The page included a variety of offenses perpetrated largely by whites, but hog theft was the largest number. He registered for World War II draft, served as private in the army. COD: cardiac arrhythmia and congestive heart failure.

Ragion (b. 1912–d. 1972); w. Virdie Singletary (b.?–d. 1984) 1932; children: James (b. 1930), Clara Green and Sallie's son Ragion (b. 1912). Ragion and Virdie had two children: son James (b. 1930), and daughter Clara (b. 1934). James died November 17, 1972, from cardiac arrest, bilateral pneumonia, and heart insufficiency. Virdie died in 1984.

CHAPTER 7: *Saving Simon Mitchell, Mitchell and Lee v. McElvin 45 Ga. 558 (1872)*

Simon Lee (b. 1827?) and Masiah Hagins (Maria) (b. 1840–d. btw. 1880 and 1900), "both freedmen," w. February 17, 1867, in Bulloch County. They had nine children: Thomas (b. 1863), Harriett (b. 1866), John Eddie (b. 1869/70–d. 1935), George (b. 1871), Sarah (b. 1872), Lula (b. 1876), Charity (b. 1879), Willie, son (b. 1883), Anderson (b. 1885–d. 1935); COD: uremia gangrene of penis and abdominal wall.

Simon Bissett aka Lee aka Mitchell (b. 1857) laborer; w. Ann (b. 1862); children: Saina (b. 1880).

Simon McElvin, in John McElvin's household as a 14-year-old farm laborer in 1870; his brother Thomas, age 21, in same household in 1870, a farm laborer.

Thomas McElvin, Simon's fellow slave (b. 1849); m. Maria Cone (b. 1858).

William W. Mitchell (b. 1840–d. 1893); w. Lydia (b. 1854–d. 1926), washerwoman; COD: cerebral hemorrhage; children: Jeanette (b. 1871), Arthur (b. 1873), huckster (1910), laborer on wharf), rented house could read but not write, on City Savannah voting rolls in 1895 when he was 22; w. Ada (b. 1883), laundress: Mary (b. 1878–d. 1880); COD: malaria; Lila (b. 1883–d. 1926), servant, cook for private family, m. John Jones, railroad flagman (b. 1882); children: William (b. 1886); Francino (b. 1886).

CHAPTER 8: *The Mysterious Fate of the Comptons and Tillmans, Brinster v. Compton 68 Ala. 299 (1880)*

Hiram Brinster, aka Bruister, aka Brewster (b. in Mississippi, 1849–d. 1917).

Friday Compton; children: Ben (b. 1861) and John (b. 1866).

John Compton (b. 1867–d. 1923); w. Cinnie Compton (b. 1875), Choctaw, Alabama, which is where the Bruisters lived; John Compton was one of the slaves whom Hiram Brinster (Bruister) wanted as his apprentice. They rented their house and farm. Also, Emily (4), Frank (15), Stephen (10) Compton lived by themselves as farm laborers in 1880. They could have been the remaining children of Friday Compton. Adopted children: William, 16 (b. 1894), who worked on the farm; Luberta, 14 (b. 1895); and Bessie Tillman, 13 (b. 1897).

Simon Tillman (b. 1863); w. Minervia (b. 1866) 1882; Julie, b. 1882), Lottie, (b. 1884), Luther, (b. 1888), Rubie, (b. 1890), William, (b. 1894), Lubirta, (b. 1895), Bessie, (b. 1896), Limmy (b. 1898), and Mollie, (b. 1900). Only the older children, Julie, Lottie and Luther, worked. They were farm laborers.

William Compton (b. 1894); w. Ada Woods; employed as 1929 tobacco worker Danville, VA; 1930, both back in Choctaw;

he a farm operator, through 1950 census; first a niece and
then her father lived with them.

Lubirta Compton (b. 1895); h. Charles Connelley; m. 1935

Julia Tillman (b. 1883); h. Horace Hatcher in 1904. Her
sisters, Willie Tillman (b. 1895–d. 1931) and Lemmie
(b. 1899), lived with Julia and Horace in 1910. By 1920,
Horace was a farmer, and Willie and Lemmy no longer
lived with them. In 1930, Horace and Julie lived in Whis-
tler and Plateau, Mobile, AL, where she was a washerwoman and he was a Methodist minister.

Willie Tillman (b. 1892–d. 1931); h. Malachia Washington (b.
1884–d. 1940). They rented their house, and he was a farm-
worker. Children: Angalo or Onzalo Roosevelt (b. 1913).
Malachia signed up for the WW I draft. Onzalo married
Naomi Ridgeway on December 31, 1933, in Lavaca in
Choctaw County. Onzalo signed up for the World War II
draft with his mother as next of kin. Willie died November
27, 1940, in Choctaw County. Onzalo served in the Coast
Guard for a year and died of "natural causes" on September 1, 1944.

Lottie Tillman (b. 1884); h. Edgar Spraggen (b. 1887) in Choctaw County.

Luther Tillman (b. 1889–d. 1935), Choctaw farm laborer.

Rubie Tillman (b. 1890), in 1910, lived with Pete and Dora
Tillman and their children. Sinnie, their daughter, 21,
married Sim Campbell (b. 1891–d. bef. 1951) in Choctaw
County in 1911; Curley, 16, and Tom, 14, their sons. Sinnie
and Sim moved to Birmingham by 1920; she was a laundress, and their niece Minnie Chaney lived with them at
age 13.

CHAPTER 9: *Violet Maples and Boss: The Family Feud That Wasn't, Maples v. Maples, 49 Miss. 393 (Miss. 1873)*

Ambrick Maples (b. 1811); w. Sarah (b. 1832): children: Violet (b. 1835), Nancy (b. 1859), Mary (b. 1861), and John (b. 1863).

Violet (b. 1835); children: Boss (b. 1858 or 1861–d. 1935), Henry (b. 1872), Lucy (b. 1876), and Tom (b. 1875).

Boss Maples (b. 1858–d. 1932, Mississippi); w. Lizzie Duncan (b. 1866) from the neighboring Duncan family; she was about 16. She disappears from the census after 1880 and perhaps passed away because Boss remarried, and her mother, Clory, and other family members remained in the neighborhood. W. Lou Jarvis (b. 1862–d. bef. 1910) in 1886; w. Carrie Strickland (b. 1884–d. 1964); occupation: housekeeping, farmwork; COD: acute thrombosis; children: Joe (b. 1910–d. 1939), occupation: Fisher Body Factory; COD: undetermined; Boss (b. 1913–d. 1995), occupation: Fisher Body Factory; farmer; last address Chicago, Cook County, IL 60621; children: Thomas (b. 1920 or 1916–d. 1992), Jordan (aka Judge) (b. 1921–d. 1987).

Joe (b. 1910–d. 1939); w. Julia.

Boss Jr. (b. 1913–d. 1995) Memphis?

Thomas (b. 1920–d. 1992); w. Georgia; w. Lora; served WWII from March 13, 1941.

Jordan (aka Judge) (b. 1921–d. 1987); w. Mildred Mathews (b. 1921–d. 2004); children: Ora Lee Maples, Merri-King.

Tom Maples (b. 1875); w. Leona Hampton (b. 1880); m. 1900; children: Clemmie (b. 1902).

Clemmie Dixon (b. 1902–d. 1970); h. Herbert Dixon: children: Bernice (Thomas) (b. 1922); Rosie (Woods) (b. 1924); Dorothy (Newsome) (b. 1929); Bessie (b. 1932); Uzzie Walker (b. 1932); Flora (Calvin) (b. 1934); Herbert Jr. (b. 1936); Tommie (b. 1939); and Gloria (b. 1941).

Nancy Bridgeforth (b. 1859), Violet's sister; h. Joe Bridgeforth (b. 1858–d. 1941) h., Joe Bridgeforth (b. 1861) (m. 1878); children: Joe Jr. (b. 1884–d. 1951); COD: bronchial pneumonia; Mary (b. 1887); Lewis (b. 1889); Carolina (b. 1892–d. 1937); COD: syphilitic paresis; Gandella (b. 1894), and Minnie (b. 1897).

Carolina Saulsberry (b. 1892–d. 1937); h., Sam Saulsberry (b. 1892); children: Melvin (b. 1913), Nancy (b. 1916), and Dawson (b. 1918).

Melvin Saulsberry; h., Cal Taylor; children: Semela (b. 1932), and Ora Jean Taylor (b. 1933).

Nancy Stockton (b. 1916); h. Thirkell Stockton; children: Thirkell Stockton Jr. (b. 1934–d. 1941), COD: bronchial pneumonia; Bobbie Jean (b. 1933–d. 1985).

Bobbie Jean Bowen; h. Jerry Bowen (b. 1924), occupation sand glass operator.

CHAPTER 10: *The Other Bridgeforths*

George Bridgeforth (b. 1838–d. 1923); w. Jennie (b. 1845–d. 1922); children: Sarah Bridgeforth Lampkin (b. 1866–d. 1923); Perthenia Bridgeforth Meals (b. 1876–d. 1920), George Ruffin (b. 1872–d. 1955), Isaac Ike (b. 1879–d. 1968), William Shirley (b. 1882–d. 1918), Bascom (b. 1887–d. 1974).

George Ruffin Bridgeforth (b. 1872–d. 1955); w. Datie Miller (b. 1880–d. 1971); children: George M. (b. 1906), Elva (b. 1910), Dodie (b. 1913), Marie (b. 1917).

Isaac (Ike) (b. 1879–d. 1968); w. Ella Stuart (b. 1884–d. 1913); children: William Sousa (b. 1907–d. 2004); w. Ila Townsend (b. 1891–d. 1982); children: Darden (b. 1920–d. 1996).

Bascom (b. 1887–d. 1974); w. Rassie Lee Townsend (b. 1888–d. 1963); children: George (b. 1910–d. 1940), Embry (b. 1913–d. 1974), William Frost (b. 1915–d. 1993); listed as white, light-brown hair with hazel eyes on Oct. 16, 1940, draft card; worked at the Aluminum Company of America (Alcoa) in Cleveland; his wife, Arnell, did private housework; Vivian (b. 1917–d. 2017); m. Ural Smith., Price (b. 1921–d. 1958), enlisted in air force December 1944, discharged March 1946; children: Bessie (b. 1923).

Price Bridgeforth (b. 1921–d. 1958), w. Lula Mae (b. 1921); children: Price W. (b. 1940–d. 1974), in army 1959–61; Joyce (b. 1945–d. 1988); Barbara (b. 1948); h. William.

Darden Bridgeforth (b. 1920–d. 1996); w. Elizabeth White (b. 1922–d. 1973); children: George Darden (b. 1939–d. 2005), Marie (b. 1941), Mildred (b. 1939), John (b. 1944), Paul (b. 1946), William Bridgeforth (b. 1948), Olivia (b. 1948), Mitchell (b. 1948), Greg (b. 1955), Bill (b. 1958).

Bill (b. 1958); children: Kyle (b. 1990), Carlton (b. 1985).

Greg (b. 1955); child: Lamont.

ACKNOWLEDGMENTS

During conversations with William "Sandy" Darity while he and Kirsten Mullen were working on their *From Here to Equality* book, I kept wondering what happened to the children and their families who were ensnared back into slavery as supposed apprentices, after the Thirteenth Amendment freed them. I knew that a few parents and occasional help from the Freedmen's Bureau freed some children. It seemed, however, that we didn't know what happened to them and their descendants afterwards. They also didn't surface in the reparations discussion.

Researching *My Face Is Black Is True: Callie House and the Struggle for Ex-Slave Reparations* (2005) and *We Are Who We Say We Are: A Black Family's Search for Home Across the Atlantic World* (2015) required a great deal of ancestry- and descendant-finding beyond my use of the National Archives in DC from decades ago when Howard University professor Elsie Lewis took students there repeatedly. The patient teaching of Sara Dunlap Jackson, one of the first black professionals at the archives, has endured and informed the work of tracing the families in this book as they sought freedom. Suggestions and materials from Rick Wilson, historian of Williamson County, Tennessee, helped in verifying why on my mother's side everyone inherited the Southall name. My Southall ancestors, enslaved and living in hardscrabble poverty, afterwards finally moved to

Nashville in adjacent Davidson County in the twentieth century where conditions were slightly better. April Davis, assistant archivist at the Limestone County (Alabama) Archives, relentlessly helped me to unearth sources on the George Bridgeforth descendants even while the pandemic kept the archives closed.

Thanks to V. P. Franklin and Melinda Chateauvert for reading and commenting on the manuscript, and to Nancy Bean and Maida Odom for their help. Everyone at Beacon was supportive as usual. Thanks to Gayatri Patnaik and Joanna Green for urging me to finish this project when, weary of dead ends, I was about to abandon it.

I'm glad I persisted in finding some more of the history of black folk, and I encourage others to continue the task of reconstruction.

NOTES

INTRODUCTION

1. Michael Grossberg, *Governing the Hearth: Law and the Family in Nineteenth-Century America* (Chapel Hill: University of North Carolina Press, 1988), 280 and notes there cited; Peter Bardaglio, "Challenging Parental Custody Rights: The Legal Reconstruction of Parenthood in the Nineteenth-Century American South," *Continuity and Change* 4 (1989): 259–91.
2. Douglas Blackmon, *Slavery by Another Name: The Re-Enslavement of Black Americans from the Civil War to World War II* (New York: Anchor Books, 2008).
3. Unless noted otherwise the information on the family history of each litigant discussed is in the appendix. Detailed data was taken largely from Ancestry.com. Material from newspapers, books, interviews, and secondary materials generally is cited in the endnotes.
4. A number of genealogists and community activists have collected local information on forced apprenticeships, mostly from Freedmen's Bureau records. In Maryland, a slave state that stayed in the Union, US Supreme Court chief justice Salmon Chase on Circuit used the Thirteenth Amendment to outlaw forced apprenticeships of the state's black freed children. *In re Turner* 24 F. Cas. 337 (C.C.D. Md. 1867). Afterwards, some planters holding children illegally released them, and the abuse gradually ended.

CHAPTER 1: THE LOST CHILDREN OF NATHAN AND JENNEY COX

1. The names are in Cox v. Jones 1866 Case File, Alabama Department of Archives and History, Montgomery, AL, pp. 5–7.
2. Cox v. Jones 1866 Case File.
3. Cox v. Jones 40 Ala. 297 (1866).
4. US, Freedmen's Bureau Records, 1865–1878, Records of the Field Offices: Complaint of Nathan Cox v. Frank Jones, June

11, 1867, referred to Mr. Crimson. Crawford Russell Gorka was given instructions to bring suit before the civil magistrate.
5. *Cox v. Jones.*

CHAPTER 2: FREEING HENRY COMAS

1. By 1860, he had thirteen females, eight ages eleven to twenty-nine, and five ages three to seven; and thirteen males, seven ages seven to twenty-seven, the others below age three.
2. Comas v. Reddish, 35 Ga. 236 (1866).
3. The 1866 Apprenticeship Act in Georgia, quote from the act in the *Comas v. Reddish.* In March 1866, under Presidential Reconstruction, Georgia, like other Southern states, passed new apprenticeship legislation amending the laws concerning apprentices. The new law was ostensibly designed to provide for the large number of "colored minors" who, because of the Civil War, were "thrown upon society, helpless from want of parental protection, want of means of support, inability to earn their daily bread, and from age and other causes." In fact, it was designed to help the planters who wanted to keep black children as unpaid labor as long as possible. The 1866 law did not "envision indenturing a colored minor in this kind of case. . . . Specifically, the law provides that in all cases where the parents are, from poverty, infirmity, from disease or old age, unable to support their minor children, the Ordinary is authorized to bind out their children." Citation and text in Georgia statutes: Acts of the General Assembly of the state of Georgia, passed in Milledgeville, at an annual session in 1865, and January, February, and March, 1866 [volume 1], https December:///dlg.usg.edu/record /dlg_zlgl_37038824/fulltext.text. TITLE II. APPRENTICES. SEC. 1. Minors may be bound out by parents. SEC. 2. By Judge of County Court or Ordinary in certain cases. SEC. 3. Indentures, how made, witnessed and kept. SEC. 4. What the Master shall teach and furnish to the apprentice. SEC. 5. Controversies. Master in default. Apprentice. SEC. 6. Relation dissolved by consent of parties. Death of the Master. [Illegible Text] to. SEC. 7. May be dissolved at instance of the master of the apprentice or his friend. SEC. 8. Proceeds of labor. Allowance to apprentice. SEC. 9. Right of action in the master. SEC. 10. Laws of force. (No. 3.) An Act to alter and amend the laws of this State, in relation to Apprentices. 1. SEC. I. The General Assembly of this State, do enact, From and after the passage of this act, that all minors may, by whichever parent has the legal control of them, be bound out as apprentices

to any respectable person, until they attain the age of twenty-one, or for a shorter period. Parents may bind out minor children. 2. SEC. II. It shall be the duty of the Judge of the County Court, or the Ordinary, to bind out, in like manner, all minors, whose parents [illegible text] dead, or whose parents reside out of the county, the profits of whose estate are insufficient for their support and maintenance; also, all minors whose parents, from age, infirmity or poverty, are unable to support them. Judge of Co. Court or Ordinary in [illegible text] [illegible text]. 3. SEC. III. Indentures of apprenticeship shall be made in duplicate, and witnessed in the same manner as deeds. The original shall be kept by the master, and the duplicate shall be filed and recorded, either in the office of the Judge of the County Court, or in the Ordinary's office, and it shall not be necessary for the apprentice to sign the same. [Illegible text] how made, witnessed and kept.

4. *Comas v. Reddish.*
5. *Comas v. Reddish.*
6. Mary Frances Berry, *My Face Is Black Is True: Callie House and the Struggle for Ex-Slave Reparations* (New York: Knopf, 2005), 10–11 and notes there cited.
7. Ira Berlin and Leslie Rowland, eds., *Families and Freedom: A Documentary History of African-American Kinship in the Civil War Era* (New York: New Press, 1997), 140–47; Freedmen's Bureau Records, F. P. Meigs, box 115; Catherine and Norman Riley, quoted in Mary Frances Berry, *My Face Is Black Is True: Callie House and the Struggle for Ex-Slave Reparations* (New York: Knopf, 2005), 10–11 and notes there cited.
8. *Comas v. Reddish.* Melissa Milewski shared a copy of the trial record from before the pandemic, which includes the testimony; see finding citation from series RG-SG-S; 92-11, Box 49, folder A-3957; Berry, *My Face Is Black Is True,* 10–11 and notes there cited. In the US census, "mulatto" was a category from 1850 to 1890 and in 1910 and 1920. "Octoroon" and "quadroon" were categories in 1890.
9. *Comas v. Reddish.* Melissa Milewski shared a copy of the trial record from before the pandemic, which includes the testimony, see finding citation from series RG-SG-S; 92-11, Box 49, folder A-3957.
10. *Comas v. Reddish.*
11. *Comas v. Reddish.* Judge Harris (1805–1876), born in Watkinsville, lived in Milledgeville, Georgia, where he opened a law office after being admitted to the bar. He served as a state

representative from Baldwin County in 1836 and again from 1845 to 1849. In 1859, he was elected judge of the Superior Court of the Ocmulgee Judicial Circuit and served until January 1866, when the state legislature elected him to the state supreme court, where he served until the adoption of the Reconstruction Constitution of 1868. He succeeded Judge Charles Jones Jenkins, who became governor. Jenkins, a Democrat, had served as attorney general of Georgia from 1831 to 1834. He then went on to serve as governor of Georgia from December 14, 1865, to January 13, 1868, when Republicans were elected to take over the state government.

12. *Comas v. Reddish.*

13. As elsewhere, settlers in Florida forcibly displaced the Seminoles and other Indigenous people. The area slightly northeast of the current city of Alachua, which was founded in 1884, was among the first settled by Americans in Florida in the early nineteenth century.

14. Georgia Death index. There is also a Henry Comas married to Emiline Blunt on May 8, 1873, in Georgia and both living in Wayne, Georgia. He died on January 2, 1926. Jincey's fate was not recorded.

15. Comas, born in 1825 in Georgia.

16. Georgia, US Death Index , 1919–1998.

CHAPTER 3: THE RESCUE OF MARY CANNON

1. *Cannon v. Stuart* 8 Del. 223 (Del. Super. Ct. 1866); Delaware, US, Marriage Records, 1744–1912.

2. See, for example, Henry Gannett, *The Origin of Certain Place Names in the United States*, 2nd ed. (Washington, DC: Government Printing Office, 1905), 98; "History," Town of Dagsboro, Delaware, 2024, https://dagsboro.delaware.gov/history.

3. Gannett, *The Origin of Certain Place Names in the United States*, 98; "History," Town of Dagsboro.

4. See, for example, a proposal in February 1862 for compensated emancipation, "The Abolition of Slavery in Delaware," *Wilmington Republican*, February 5, 1862; Samuel died in 1842 according to Find a Grave; Molly Murray, "Archivist Unearths Document Listing Last Sussex Slave Owners," *Delaware Online*, May 12, 2016, https://www.delawareonline.com/story/news/local/2016/05/12/archivest-unearths-document-listing-last-sussex-slave-owners/84255486; also "Slavery in Delaware," Slavery in the North, 2003, http://slavenorth.com/delaware.htm.

5. John Cannon (b. 1833–d. 1880), US Civil War Draft Registra-
tions, Records 1863–1865, First Delaware Infantry Regiment,
Vols. 2–5.
6. Julie Zauzmer Weil, Adrian Blanco, and Leo Dominguez, "More
Than 1,800 Congressmen Once Enslaved Black People. This Is
Who They Were, and How They Shaped the Nation," *Washington Post*, January 10, 2022.
7. Sussex County Delaware Genealogy and History, http://genealo-
gytrails.com/del/sussex/bios_sc_h1.html.
8. The quotes are taken from the court report; Cannon v. Stuart 8
Del. 223 (Del. Super. Ct. 1866).
9. *Middletown Transcript*, October 29, 1870, p. 2, correspondence
of the *Wilmington Gazette* from Millsboro, Delaware, April 24,
1875.
10. She was still living in the family home in Sussex in 1910. She
moved into Palmer Home retirement home in Kent sometime
thereafter and died there at age eighty-two in 1912; US Death
Records, 1861–1933.
11. *Middletown Transcript*, October 29, 1870, p. 2, correspondence
of the *Wilmington Gazette* from Millsboro, Delaware, April 24,
1875.
12. 1870 Federal Census, Dagsboro Hundred, Sussex, Delaware,
Roll M593A.
13. 1880 Federal Census, Dagsboro Hundred, Sussex, Delaware,
Roll 117, p. 516D, Enumeration District 049.
14. Public Archives Commission, Delaware Public Archives, Dover,
Delaware, Marriage 1744–1912, Year 1883, Record Group R.G.
1325.003; 1900 Federal Census, Dagsboro Hundred, Sussex,
Delaware, Roll p. 8, Enumeration District 0089 1240057; Howard (b. 1883), Joshua (b. 1885), Minnie (b. 1887), Mary E. (b.
1886), Ernest (b. 1891), Gertrude (b. 1897), and Cutie (b. 1897).
15. 1910 Federal Census, Dagsboro Hundred, Sussex, Delaware,
Roll p. T624, p. 20B, Enumeration District 0016.
16. Delaware Public Archives, Delaware US Land Records 1677–1947,
Roll No. 139; Abstracts of Wills, Sussex County, Delaware
1700s to 1800s, Probate Place, Sussex, Delaware.
17. *Wilmington Evening Journal*, September 26 and October 4,
1917.
18. 1920 Federal Census, Dagsboro Hundred, Sussex, Delaware,
Roll T 625-201, p. 19B, Enumeration District 193; Delaware
Public Archives, Dover, Vital Records 1800-1933, Series No.
Death Certificates 23.

CHAPTER 4: THE EMANCIPATION OF ELIZA AND HARRIET AMBROSE

1. Jonathan Spiers, "Black History Month: The Story of Lucy Ross," *Port City Daily* (Wilmington, NC), February 23, 2014, https://portcitydaily.com/local-news/2014/02/23/black-history -month-the-story-of-lucy-ross.

2. Hoke P. Kimball and Bruce Henson, *Governor's* [sic] *Houses and State Houses of British Colonial America, 1607–1783* (Jefferson, NC: McFarland and Co., 2017), 238.

3. In the Matter of Harriet Ambrose and Eliza Ambrose, 61 N.C. 91 (N.C. 1867).

4. Mary Farmer-Kaiser, *Freedwomen and the Freedmen's Bureau: Race, Gender and Public Policy in the Age of Emancipation* (New York: Fordham University Press, 2010), 122–25, freed-women "to put forth almost superhuman efforts to regain their children."

5. Karin L. Zipf, *Labor of Innocents: Forced Apprenticeship in North Carolina, 1715–1919* (Baton Rouge: Louisiana State University Press, 2005), 97–99.

6. Farmer-Kaiser, *Freedwomen and the Freedmen's Bureau.*

7. *In the Matter of Harriet Ambrose and Eliza Ambrose.*

8. In analyzing North Carolina Supreme Court cases about apprenticeship from 1867 to 1924, Karin L. Zipf shows that the shifting legal results are derived from gradual widespread changes in social attitudes not only about apprenticeship but also about race, gender, and class. *Labor of Innocents,* 97–99.

9. Farmer-Kaiser, *Freedwomen and the Freedmen's Bureau.*

10. Farmer-Kaiser, *Freedwomen and the Freedmen's Bureau.*

11. Zipf concludes, in an opinion written by a Republican justice, that revoked court-ordered indentures had been made without the apprentice being in court. The head of the Freedmen's Bureau in the state adopted this latter policy. It was common custom in North Carolina, although not found in any statute, that a white child could only be apprenticed above the age of fourteen with parental consent, because the child was of an age where he or she could contribute to family income. Zipf, *Labor of Innocents,* 103–4; see also Farmer-Kaiser, *Freedwomen and the Freedmen's Bureau.*

12. Miles Mitchell v. Marina Mitchell and Her Children, 67 N.C. 307, 1872, https://case-law.vlex.com/vid/mitchell-v-mitchell -893353796.

13. *Mitchell v. Mitchell.*

14. Reade also noted there had not been a grand jury complaint that
would have adduced facts and, further, there is "no complaint
from any person except from him who wants their services. It is
not surprising that he should want them bound, because thereby
he would get services worth $150 a year *now*, and constantly
increasing in value. For these services he would make no return
to the mother, who had the burden of supporting them, and no
return to the children, except such education as they can get
at the public schools. This would seem to be great injustice to
the mother and great hardship upon the children, to say nothing of the impolicy of breaking up the domestic relations when
there is no public necessity for it." Reade explained further that
the apprenticeship code, "if understood literally, will embrace
almost all the orphan children in the State. Since the wreck of
fortunes by the war, it is a rare case where a fatherless child can
be educated and maintained out of the profits of its estate alone.
But still, when the family is kept together and industry and economy are added to a small income from property, the children
may be provided for in the domestic forum. The public does not
become interested to break up these relations unless the children are likely to become chargeable upon the parish, or unless
their moral or physical condition requires a change." *Mitchell v.
Mitchell.*
15. "Judge Russell's Letter of Declination," Democratic State Executive Committee, Doc. No. 1–1888, "Democracy vs. Radicalism,"
Hand-Book of N.C. Politics for 1888 (Raleigh: E. M. Uzzell
Printer, 1888).
16. Mary Frances Berry, *Black Resistance/White Law: A History
of Constitutional Racism in America* (1971; revised ed.: New
York: Penguin Books, 1994), 94–96. In a widely reported speech
during the summer of 1898, a Georgia woman, Rebecca Ann
Felton, openly called for lynching as the appropriate response to
the threat she claimed black men posed to white women. Alex-
ander Manly answered her speech with an editorial in the *Daily
Record* in which he noted the historical prevalence of the rape of
black women by Southern white men and pointed out that many
white women were attracted to and fell in love with black men
whom they associated with by choice. The response to Manly's
editorial was reprinted in newspapers across North Carolina.
17. "Primary Source: Letter from an African American Citizen of
Wilmington to the President," November 13, 1898, available at

Anchor: A North Carolina History Online Resource, www
.ncpedia.org/anchor/primary-source-letter-3.
18. Berry, *Black Resistance/White Law*, 118. The *New York Times*
story did not report the setting, which was organized to run
blacks and Republican officeholders out of town.
19. Berry, *Black Resistance/White Law*, 94–96.

CHAPTER 5: FIGHTING FOR THE SONS OF SAMUEL AND OLIVER ADAMS
1. Adams v. Adams 36 Ga. 236 (1867).
2. *Adams v. Adams.*
3. W. E. B. Du Bois, *The Souls of Black Folk: Essays and Sketches*
(Chicago: A. C. McClurg, 1903), 92–94, 96, 100.
4. *Adams v Adams.*
5. 1860 Georgia slave population schedules, Georgia Archives; "Albany, 1910. Vason home built in 1855 by Judge David A. Vason
is located at 405 North Monroe Street," https://vault.georgia
archives.org/digital/collection/vg2/id/5167.
6. *Adams v. Adams.*
7. *Adams v. Adams.*
8. *Adams v. Adams.*
9. *Adams v. Adams.*
10. He and his wife, Rebecca, thirty-seven, whom he married in
1888; had seven children: He owned a farm with a mortgage.
Zachary, reportedly, could read and write, but no one else in the
household did. Zach was a farmer working on his own account;
his wife was Elizabeth Adams in 1930. His daughter Anice, who
married Milford Adison, was a forty-one-year-old domestic. Anice's death certificate: Georgia, US, Death Records, 1914–1940;
Anice Anderson, Georgia State Board of Health, State File No.
26010; father Zach Adams; COD: "Child birth after Convulsions Dr. Called but never came."
11. Du Bois, *The Souls of Black Folk.*
12. Adams v. McKay 36 Ga. 440 (1867) adjourned term.
13. On the 1861 England Census.
14. *Adams v. McKay.*
15. Rubin Maxwell Sinins, *Justices of the Ex-Confederate State Supreme Courts, 1860–1900: Biographical Sketches and Resource
Guide*, Vol. I (1990), and notes there cited.
16. Opinion by Walker State Supreme Court 36 Ga. 440 (1867), The
Act of March 17th, 1866, (pamph. Acts, p. 6).
17. Lee W. Formwalt, "The Camilla Massacre of 1868: Racial Violence as Political Propaganda," *Georgia Historical Quarterly* 71
(1987): 399–426, 416.

18. 1880 non-population US Census schedule. They did not hire
laborers but worked the land themselves along with family
members.

CHAPTER 6: THE CASE OF SARAH LACY

1. Pope's trial court testimony in Timmins v. Lacy, 30 Tex. 115
(1867), https://cite.case.law/tex/30/115/; Giuliana Perrone,
"'Back into the Days of Slavery': Freedom, Citizenship, and the
Black Family in the Reconstruction-Era Courtroom," *Law and
History Review* 37, no. 1 (February 2019): 125–61, notes 63–69.
Even if Harry actually thought she "had a child by another
negro," as the judge's summation of his testimony said, it was
not unusual for slaves who could not legally marry and who
escaped, were sold, or suffered other abuses of the institution
to have serial relationships and children by different parents as
a result. It seems that the proceedings include Mrs. Timmins's
statement that he was sold away.
2. *Timmins v. Lacy*. Robert was James Robert, born in 1846.
3. James Timmins, "Texas, U.S. Will and Probate Records,
1833-1974"; date of death 1859.
4. Clint Smith, *How the Word Is Passed: A Reckoning with the
History of Slavery Across America* (New York: Little, Brown,
2021); DeNeen L. Brown, "After Juneteenth, Many Black People
in Texas Remained Enslaved," *Washington Post*, June 19, 2022;
Barry Crouch, "'To Enslave the Rising Generation': The Freedmen's Bureau and the Texas Black Code," in *The Freedmen's
Bureau and Reconstruction: Reconsiderations*, ed. Paul Cim-
bala and Randall Miller (New York: Fordham University Press,
1999), 261 and notes there cited.
5. Oliver Otis Howard, *Autobiography of Oliver Otis Howard,
Major General, United States Army: Volume 2* (New York:
Baker & Taylor, 1908); Crouch, "'To Enslave the Rising Generation,'" 261 and notes there cited.
6. William A. Darity and A. Kirsten Mullen, *From Here to Equality: Reparations for Black Americans in the Twenty-First Century* (Chapel Hill: University of North Carolina Press, 2022),
Kindle ed., chapter 9 and fn 56 et seq 366 notes to pages 184–87.
For the narrative written by captain and sub-assistant commander Samuel C. Sloan to Lieutenant Madden asserting that
Texas's white supremacists sought to re-enslave the freedmen,
see Crouch, "'To Enslave the Rising Generation,'" 261.
7. Indenture filed in Cherokee District Court reported in *Timmins
v. Lacy*.

8. "They were at Harmon Carlton's during 1866 and had $50 or $60 worth of provisions left at the end of the year. The Lacys were at William Parks in 1867 who paid Moses $10 per month for meals and a house to live in with Sarah permitted to keep any wages she made separately. The Lacys insisted that with help from their children, the family would be self-sufficient and 'there would be no danger of Elkin becoming a tax on the county.'" They explained that "after securing homes for themselves for the year 1867," their employer hired the children out "to competent men, for reasonable wages, besides their necessary food, clothing and medical attention in case of sickness." They had "hired out Elkin to H. Carlton for $40, for the year 1867, food and clothing furnished, and her other boy (Chuff) to E. Morgan for $30, for the same time, and food and clothing furnish; the girl, Leney, to John T. Murray, for $35, and food, clothing, and medical bill paid." Testimony of Moses and Sarah Lacy summarized in their appeal in Timmins v. Lacy 30 Tex. 115 (1867).
9. *Timmins v. Lacy.*
10. "Lynching of Leonard Johnson," Lynching in Texas, https://www.lynchingintexas.org/items/show/522, accessed April 10, 2024.
11. *Timmins v. Lacy.*
12. E. R. Bills, *The 1910 Slocum Massacre: An Act of Genocide in East Texas* (Charleston, SC: History Press, 2014).

CHAPTER 7: SAVING SIMON MITCHELL
1. Mitchell and Lee v. McElvin 45 Ga. 558 (1872).
2. *Mitchell and Lee v. McElvin.*
3. Hugh McCall, *The History of Georgia: Containing Brief Sketches of the Most Remarkable Events up to the Present Day, 1784* (1811).
4. Robert E. Perdue, "The Negro in Savannah, 1865-1900," PhD diss., University of Georgia, 1971, pp. 124–25; John W. Blassingame, "Before the Ghetto: The Making of the Black Community in Savannah, Georgia, 1865–1880," *Journal of Social History* 6 (1973): 463–88.
5. Savannah, Georgia, US Licenses and Bonds, 1837–1909, record date 1860–1871.
6. William Harden, "Julian Schley," Chatham County, Georgia, Archives, Biographies, http://files.usgwarchives.net/ga/chatham/bios/gbs221schley.txt; the 1870 US Census recorded Simon and his brother Thomas, age twenty-one, as black farm laborers, last name McElvin.

7. Anderson's cause of death was uremia gangrene of the penis and abdominal wall.
8. *Mitchell and Lee v. McElvin.*
9. National Cyclopedia of American Biography (NATCAB); Memorial of Judge William Watts Montgomery in Volume 100, Georgia Supreme Court Reports, "Rubin Maxwell Sinins," Justices of the Ex-Confederate State Supreme Courts: Biographical Sketches and Resource Guide, 1990 research paper in my possession.
10. *Mitchell and Lee v. McElvin.*
11. *Mitchell and Lee v. McElvin*; Simon Mitchell's father, Simon Lee, born in 1824 and Masiah Hagins (Maria), born in 1840, "both freedmen," married on February 17, 1867, in Bulloch County. They had nine children.
12. Blassingame, "Before the Ghetto."
13. Blassingame, "Before the Ghetto."
14. September 18, 1894, court date for a Lydia Mitchell and Mary Mason, who were fined for having their "yards in a filthy and unsanitary condition. 200 dollars and five days in prison each"; note that Mason remitted $200. The Mayor's Fine and Information Docket for 1894–1897 records a court date of July 7, 1897, for Lydia Mitchell for disorderly conduct for assaulting and stabbing witnesses Marnie Jones, "colored," and Alice Butler, "colored," with a fork in Duffy Street Lane, 8 p.m., July 6, 1897. Lydia Mitchell was discharged. It's not clear if this is William's widow, Lydia, since there are no addresses in the record of the Mayor's Fine and Information Docket 1896–97, Savannah, GA, US Court Records, 1790–1934.
15. Judge A. H. McDonnel, Savannah, Georgia, US Court Records, 1790–1934.
16. Savannah, 121 E. Bolton; date of birth 1856; Jacob Glover and Catherine Williams, parents, Georgia State Board of Health, Bureau of Vital Statistics, standard certificate of death.
17. Local court docket. There were several charges against Simon Mitchell, all published in the *Savannah Morning News*, April 30, 1871 (last on the list of persons charged), March 22, 1884, 6:30 p.m., disorderly conduct (2nd on court list), fighting in the streets thereby creating a disturbance, a stabbing incident, no death, sentenced December 21, 1875 (1st on the list); in 1885, disorderly conduct and fighting in the streets; September 26, 1890, causing a disturbance and having a concealed weapon in a house on Jones Street, $7 or fifteen days, turned over to

city court. In 1897 (reported December 28, *Savannah Morning News*), disorderly conduct fighting in the streets. No further record of court proceedings was found on these cases in the local court or newspapers. A Simon Mitchell, born in 1851, died on July 7, 1923, in Savannah.

18. August 8, 1880, *Morning News*; *Mitchell and Lee v. McElvin*.

19. Georgia, US, Property Tax Digest, 1882–1887.

20. Clement Charlton Moseley, *The Hodges Family Murders and the Lynching of Paul Reed and Will Cato* (Statesboro, GA: Bulloch County Historical Society, 2018); Charlton Moseley and Frederick Brogdon, "A Lynching at Statesboro: The Story of Paul Reed and Will Cato," *Georgia Historical Quarterly* 65 (1981): 104–18; Mary Frances Berry, *Black Resistance/White Law: A History of Constitutional Racism in America* (New York: Appleton-Century Crofts, 1971; revised ed.: New York: Penguin Books, 1995), 125–26.

21. Berry, *Black Resistance/White Law*, 125.

22. Berry, *Black Resistance/White Law*, 125–26.

23. Berry, *Black Resistance/White Law*.

24. Berry, *Black Resistance/White Law*.

CHAPTER 8: THE MYSTERIOUS FATE OF THE COMPTONS AND TILLMANS

1. The last name is variously spelled most often Brinster or Bruister in the census and other records, and newspapers.

2. Brinster v. Compton 68 Ala. 299 (1880).

3. William Warren Rogers Sr. and Robert David Ward, *August Reckoning: Jack Turner and Racism in Post Civil War Alabama* (Tuscaloosa: University of Alabama Press, 2004), 33.

4. Chief Judge Peck on apprenticeship in *Owen v. State*, 48 Alabama 328 (1872).

5. *Owen v. State*.

6. *Owen v. State*.

7. *Owen v. State*.

8. "The Murder of Jack Turner," *New York Times*, August 28, 1882.

9. Reported widely, including in "A Scheme to Murder the People of a Whole County," *True Citizen* (Waynesboro, GA), September 1, 1882; "Uprising of Negroes Checked," *Montgomery Advertiser*, August 22, 1882; "The Choctaw Conspiracy: Exact Copies of the Papers," *Montgomery Advertiser*, August 27, 1882.

10. Holland Cotter, "A Memorial to the Lingering Horror of Lynching," *New York Times*, June 1, 2018, www.nytimes.com/2018

/06/01/arts/design/national-memorial-for-peace-and-justice
-montgomery-alabama.html, has an excellent description of the
pavilion, including the notice for Jack Turner.

11. William Warren Rogers and Robert David Ward, *August Reckoning: Jack Turner and Racism in Post–Civil War Alabama*
(Baton Rouge: University of Alabama Press, 1973); "Lynched by
Vigilantes," *St. Louis Daily Globe-Democrat*, August 22, 1882.
Because the 1890 US Census was burned, the next census was
1900, in which there is a second John Compton of Alabama, not
likely to be a Friday Compton descendant. This John Compton
is in Linden, Marengo County; married in 1886 to Margaret
Compton. He was thirty-three and she, thirty-seven, with a
four-year-old son, Daniel.

12. Julie, seventeen (1882); Lottie, fifteen (1884); Luther, eleven
(1888); Rubie, nine (1890); William, five (1894); Lubirta, four
(1895); Bessie, three (1896); Limmy, one (1898); and Mollie, two
and a half.

13. There was also a Minervia Chaney Tillman, who died March
1939 in Dallas County, Alabama, but she was married to Frank
Tillman and living in Liberty Hill, Dallas County, in 1920. She
was forty-one, born in 1872. He was fifty-four, and they had a
five-year-old daughter, Aretha. He was a farm laborer.

14. World War I draft registration card, according to the Danville,
Virginia, City Directory, 1929.

CHAPTER 9: VIOLET MAPLES AND BOSS

1. There was only one other case that involved an apprentice
reported by the Mississippi Supreme Court in 1873: Howry v.
Calloway, 48 Miss. 587.

2. "A Brief History of DeSoto County, Mississippi," About DeSoto
County, DeSoto County Geneological [sic] Society, https://www
.desotocountyms.gov/DocumentCenter/View/56/History-of
-DeSoto-County?bidId=. Ames married Sarah Carrie Rush in
1869; she was apparently the mother of his children born earlier.

3. In 1873, when *Maples v. Maples* was decided, Ambrick worked
in DeSoto County on the Jeffries plantation near Horn Lake. A
lovely house with arches, it burnt down in 1977; Chris Edwards
and Faye Axford, in "An Introduction to County Architecture,"
by Robert Gamble, in *The Lure and Lore of Limestone County:
Containing a History and Genealogical Material of More Than
Two Hundred Houses of the Nineteenth Century* (New Orleans: Portals Press/Limestone County Historical Society, 1978),

97–98. The marriage certificate seems to identify McWilliams as "Fed."

4. Thomas O. (1826–1910). The Bridgeforths from the Desoto Museum were this Thomas and his wife, Carline Gray (1833–1857).

5. R. J. Jeffries's place is where some of the discussion took place between Ambrick and the Bridgeforths.

6. The 1880 US Census recorded Violet Maples, born in 1835, as widowed, age forty-five.

7. He was probably referring to William Maples, Malcolm Maples's brother, who migrated to Louisiana and then Mississippi. In cases where a freed child was claimed by a white former slave owner, the child would usually state how content they were to stay where they were expressing no complaint.

8. As discussed later, Joe was not as lucky as R. L.'s brother John's "mulatto" child, George, who, helped by his father, became prosperous after slavery.

9. Other parents found their children alone and then had them taken and asked the bureau for help in retrieving them. Some children were impressed by their captor to claim their parents unfit or abusive and insist they wanted to stay with the abductor. The bureau would offer transportation home but to no avail. Wilma King, *Stolen Childhood: Slave Youth in Nineteenth-Century America* (Bloomington: Indiana University Press, 1997), 144–47.

10. Maples v. Maples 49 Miss. 393 (1873).

11. Melissa Ditmore, *Unbroken Chains: The Hidden Role of Human Trafficking in the American Economy* (Boston: Beacon Press, 2023).

12. *Index to Miscellaneous Documents of the House of Representatives for First Session of the Forty-Eighth Congress, 1883–84. In Forty Volumes,* Vol. 19 (Washington, DC: Government Printing Office, 1884); Van H. Manning won.

13. Lou and Boss had no reported children. Sometime before the 1910 US Census, Lou Jarvis apparently died, and Boss later married Carrie Strickland from nearby Lake Cormorant in DeSoto County.

14. No marriage record has been found for Boss and Carrie.

15. Fisher Body opened in 1936; certificate of death state of Tennessee; his brother Judge was the informant. Joe and Julia lived at 824 Randle Street; death certificate shows his mother's maiden name was Carrie Strickland, born in Goldwater, Mississippi; certificate of death, Tennessee, December 20, 1939; Joe's mother,

Carrie, fifty-eight, and brother Judge (Jordan), twenty, lived with him and his wife, Georgia, seventeen. The two men were laborers, and their mother described herself as a farm laborer, the work she always did during her life. Carrie died March 17, 1964, from acute thrombosis in Memphis.

16. 1930 US census; Tennessee Death Certificate, no. 879, February 23, 1937; Joe and Nancy's daughter, Carolina Saulsberry, born in 1893, worked as a domestic until her death in Memphis from syphilitic paresis, in 1937, at age forty-four. She could read and write and was married to Sam Saulsberry. Their daughter, Melvin (aka Malvin) was born in 1913; a daughter, Nancy, age fourteen, was born in 1916; and a son, Dawson, age twelve, was born in 1918. A boarder, Winfield Scott, age eighty-two, also stayed with them. They lived at 494 Alston Avenue in Memphis.

17. Mississippi Wills and Probate Records, July 10, 1941, 1780–1982, DeSoto, Case Number 6591, Will Record, Vols. 4–6, 1918–1957, Mississippi.

18. Mississippi Wills and Probate Records, July 10, 1941. Solomon Payne was Joe's executor.

19. Alabama Department of Archives and History, Limestone, Estate Case Files, Bridgeforth, R. L.—Byrd William, 1865–1915. Upon R. L.'s death his half-brother, who lived at his house reported his death to County probate judge James Horton and estimated his estate at either 400,000 or 400.00 depending on how his scribble is perceived. The fact that over the next years thereafter the file cited shows consistent payments to various providers and other business transactions well above 400.00 before the estate was formally drawn down and closed makes it more likely that the amount is considerably more.

20. As recorded in the official Alabama Death Index.

21. Tom Maples, born in 1875, in Alabama, not likely Boss's brother, was counted as a lodger in Joseph Edemy's household, St. Louis Ward 17, Saint Louis City, Missouri, in 1910. and was a porter on a steam car. He was a widower. Edemy was a porter in a shoe factory. He and his wife and mother-in-law had six other lodgers, two adult females and four males. The women had no occupation listed, but one man was a janitor in a shirt factory, another a porter in a saloon, another a laborer in a gas house; the seventeen-year- old male had no occupation listed.

22. When the black lung benefit program was established by the Federal Coal Mine and Safety Act of 1969. Herbert Dixon started to receive monthly benefit payments, according to his

granddaughter Theresa, who calls it "Black lung money." Apparently, he remarried after Clemmie died.

23. Interview with Gloria's daughter Dr. Theresa Dixon Taylor, July 4, 2023.

24. Gilda Williams, "Hispanic Named to Park Post," *Harvey Markham Star*, February 24, 1996.

25. Letters to the editor, *Harvey Star*, June 23, 1996.

26. Dave Fanno, "Voters Shift Power in Harvey," *Harvey Star*, April 18, 1999. On May 3, 1998, Dixon's photograph in the *Harvey Star* showed her with officials at the remodeled Holmes Recreation Center in her Park district.

CHAPTER 10: THE OTHER BRIDGEFORTHS

1. A lovely house with arches, it burnt down in 1977. Chris Edwards and Faye Axford, in "An Introduction to County Architecture," by Robert Gamble, *The Lure and Lore of Limestone County: Containing a History and Genealogical Material of More Than Two Hundred Houses of the Nineteenth Century* (New Orleans: Portals Press/Limestone County Historical Society, 1978), 97–98.

2. The Bridgeforth Farms website, https://bridgeforthfarms.com /about/history, has a good outline of the George Bridgeforth descendants' presentation of their history with photographs. In 1880, relatively few blacks (approximately 12 percent) had acquired plots of forty acres or more; instead, most black men worked as sharecroppers or wage laborers.

3. Massachusetts Agricultural College is now the University of Massachusetts Amherst.

4. His father and mother, George and Jennie, held forty-one shares, while his brothers Ike, William, and Bascom together controlled forty-four shares. George Ruffin and his wife, Datie, owned eighty-nine shares, making them the largest shareholders. August Meier, *Negro Thought in America: 1880–1915* (Ann Arbor: University of Michigan Press, 1970), 143.

5. Nancy Anne Carden, "A Study of Southern Black Landownership, 1865–1940: The Bridgeforth Family of Limestone County, Alabama," master's thesis, University of Tennessee, 1990, p. 33.

6. This was when Robert and Price Hendricks, white landowners, traded a tract of land on the Tennessee River. Carden, "A Study of Southern Black Landownership, 1865–1940," p. 33, and notes there cited. Rev. Albert Cleage founded the shrine of the black Madonna in Detroit bought a farm that they called Beulah

Land, in northwest South Carolina along the Georgia border. Since Reverend Cleage died, in 1999, the project has struggled to remain afloat. "The Beulah Land Story," Shrines of the Black Madonna, https://theyearofrestoration.org/the-beulah-land -story. The song has remained one of many black freedom songs but not much emphasized.

7. Carden, "A Study of Southern Black Landownership," 35–36 and notes there cited.

8. Carden, "A Study of Southern Black Landownership," chapter 3, p. 36, and notes there cited.

9. The discussion of the Bridgeforths and the New Deal is based on Nancy Anne Carden, "Beulahland and the New Deal 1920–1940," chapter 4 and notes there cited, in Carden, "A Study of Southern Black Landownership"; Nancy L. Grant, *TVA and Black Americans: Planning for the Status Quo* (Philadelphia: Temple University Press, 1990).

10. Carden, "A Study of Southern Black Landownership," 35–36; Grant, *TVA and Black Americans*.

11. Alabama US Convict Records 1886–1952, Bascomb Bridgeforth, Limestone, Vol. 12, Alabama Department of Archives and History, Archive Roll No. SG007468; maximum would have been to November 17, 1928.

12. William "Sou" Bridgeforth, "The Brief Life and Grateful Times of William Sou Bridgeforth," July 2001.

13. United States of America v. William S. Bridgeforth, Helen Bridgeforth, and Universal Life Insurance Company, 1959 U.S. Dist. LEXIS 4333, 59-1 U.S. Tax Cas. (CCH) P9447 3 A.F.T.R.2d (RIA) 1292; "U.S. Sues to Collect 52,608 in Taxes," *Nashville Tennessean*, October 18, 1961. Since 1951, federal law has required gamblers to register with the Internal Revenue Service, buy a $50 gambling-tax stamp, and pay a 10 percent excise tax on their annual gross bets.

14. "U.S. Predicts Payoff Probe Indictments," *Nashville Tennessean*, February 10, 1964.

15. "Court Order Sets Mortgage Payment," *Nashville Tennessean*, January 22, 1965; 1965 U.S. Dist. LEXIS 9350 66-1 U.S. Tax Cas. (CCH) P9410 17 A.F.T.R.2d (RIA) 800.

16. Bridgeforth, "The Brief Life and Grateful Times of William Sou Bridgeforth"; Dwight Lewis, "Negro Leagues Owner William Bridgeforth Dies," *Nashville Tennessean*, July 25, 2004.

17. Register of Prisoners Committed to County Jail, p. 14. Darden was committed on August 24, 1941, until December 3, 1941;

when he was found guilty, he was bound over to the grand jury
when his case was reversed and remanded by the state supreme
court; Limestone County archives.

18. *Bridgeforth v. State* 10 So. 2d. 744 (Ala. 1942).
19. *Alabama Courier*, October 4, 1945, and November 1, 1945.
20. *Alabama Courier*, April 3, 1947; *Decatur Daily*, April 20, 1947.
21. "Socially Disadvantaged, Beginning, Limited Resource, and
    Female Farmers and Ranchers," Economic Research Service,
    US Department of Agriculture, last updated January 29, 2024,
    https://www.ers.usda.gov/topics/farm-economy/socially
    -disadvantaged-beginning-limited-resource-and-female-farmers
    -and-rancher.
22. Conversations with John Boyd during 2021 and with Carl-
    ton Bridgeforth; Lisa Held, "Farm Credit Can Make or Break
    Farms. Should It Be More Equitable?" *Civil Eats*, June 5, 2003,
    https://civileats.com/2023/06/05/farm-credit-can-make-or-break
    -farms-should-it-be-more-equitable. In addition, for years, for
    black farmers, one loan source stands out as particularly signif-
    icant: the nation's Farm Credit system, which is now the coun-
    try's largest farm lender, providing 44 percent of farm loans.
    It's not a federal agency but a government-sponsored enterprise
    (GSE) that gives tax advantages and better terms with federal
    backing, like some other federal programs like housing mort-
    gages or student loans, for example. Unnoticed, it has been
    largely inaccessible to black and Indigenous farmers, for exam-
    ple. Now, Farm Credit is the focus of growing scrutiny, a result
    of its opposition to a new rule—referred to as 1071—that would
    require small business lenders to collect and report detailed
    demographic data on its borrowers.

CONCLUSION

1. See, for example, Nikole Hannah-Jones, *The 1619 Project: A
   New Origin Story*, an anthology of essays and poetry, pub-
   lished by Random House's One World imprint on November
   16, 2021. It is a book-length expansion of the essays presented
   in the 1619 Project issue of the *New York Times Magazine* in
   August 2019; Mary Frances Berry, *Black Resistance/White
   Law: A History of Constitutional Racism in America* (New
   York: Appleton-Century Crofts, 1971; revised ed.: New York:
   Penguin Books, 1995).
2. William Darity and Kirsten Mullen, *From Here to Equality:
   Reparations for Black Americans in the Twenty-First Century*
   (Chapel Hill: University of North Carolina Press, 2020).

3. Mary Frances Berry, *My Face Is Black Is True: Callie House and the Struggle for Ex-Slave Reparations* (New York: Knopf, 2006).
4. Darity and Mullen, *From Here to Equality*, 44.
5. The case is Students for Fair Admissions, Inc. v. President and Fellows of Harvard College and Students for Fair Admissions v. University of North Carolina et al., decided June 29, 2023. Jackson was addressing ante, at 55 (THOMAS, J., concurring).
6. Peter Bardaglio, "Challenging Parental Custody Rights: The Legal Reconstruction of Parenthood in the Nineteenth-Century American South," *Continuity and Change* 4 (1989): 259–91. Comas v. Reddish, 35 Ga. 236 (1866) 237–38; Lowry v. Holden, 41 Miss. 410 (1867); and other cases in which black parents regained custody of their children after they had been apprenticed include Adams v. Adams, 36 Ga. 236 (1867); Adams v. McKay, 36 Ga. 440 (1867); Hatcher v. Cutts, 42 Ga. 616 (1871); Mitchell v. McElvin, 45 Ga. 558 (1872); and Mitchell v. Mitchell, 67 N.C. 307 (1872).
7. James Barron, "New York Today," *New York Times*, October 25, 2022.
8. Dorothy Roberts, *Torn Apart: How the Child Welfare System Destroys Black Families—and How Abolition Can Build a Safer World* (New York: Basic Books, 2022).
9. Connecticut v. Belcher, SC 20531 (2022); Elizabeth Becker, "As Ex-Theorist on Young 'Superpredators,' Bush Aide Has Regrets," *New York Times*, February 9, 2001; Kristin Henning, *The Rage of Innocence: How America Criminalizes Black Youth* (New York: Pantheon, 2022); Larry DeWitt, "The Decision to Exclude Agricultural and Domestic Workers from the 1935 Social Security Act," *Social Security Bulletin* 70, no. 4 (2010), in retirement and disability policy, titled SSA, w.ssa .gov/policy/docs/ssb/v70n4/v70n4p49.html; the 1950 and 1954 amendments first included domestic service and farm labor.
10. State of Connecticut v. Keith Belcher, SC 20531 (Conn. Jan. 21, 2022).
11. Henning, *The Rage of Innocence*.
12. Robert Fogel and Stanley Engermann, *Time on the Cross: The Economics of American Negro Slavery* (New York: Norton, 1974).
13. James B. Stewart, "Industrial Slavery and Diet Deprivation: Expanding the Case for Black Reparations," in *Reparations and Reparatory Justice: Past, Present, and Future*, ed. Sundiata Keita Cha-Jua, Mary Frances Berry, and V. P. Franklin (Urbana: University of Illinois Press, 2024).

14. Leah Boustan and Ran Abramitzky, *Streets of Gold: America's Untold Story of Immigrant Success* (New York: PublicAffairs, 2022).

15. Stewart, "Industrial Slavery and Diet Deprivation."

16. Luther Adams, *Way Up North in Louisville: African American Migration in the Urban South, 1930–1970* (Chapel Hill: University of North Carolina Press, 2010).

17. Boustan and Abramitzky, *Streets of Gold*; Leah Boustan, *Competition in the Promised Land: Black Migrants in Northern Cities and Labor Markets* (Princeton, NJ: Princeton University Press, 2016).

18. Also, when the Atlantic Slave Trade was declared illegal by Britain in 1807 and by the Dutch, French, Spanish, and Portuguese, thereafter, slave traders whose contracts became void were compensated but the captured Africans were not.